# PEOPLE RESOURCING

## CIPD REVISION GUIDE 2005

**Dr Ted Johns** has been a CIPD Chief Examiner for about 20 years and is currently Chief Examiner for both People Resourcing and Managing People. He is an experienced author with a number of publishers.

**Charles Leatherbarrow** is a Senior Lecturer in HRM at Staffordshire University. He teaches a wide range of undergraduate and postgraduate HRM modules, including the CIPD People Resourcing module. Prior to h̶ for over 18 yeaɪ nager.

The Chartered Institute of Personnel and Development is the leading
publisher of books and reports for personnel and training professionals,
students, and all those concerned with the effective management and
development of people at work. For details of all our titles, please
contact the publishing department:

*tel:* 020 8263 3387

*fax:* 020 8263 3850

*e-mail:* publish@cipd.co.uk

The catalogue of all CIPD titles can be viewed on the CIPD website:

www.cipd.co.uk/bookstore

# PEOPLE RESOURCING

## CIPD REVISION GUIDE 2005

### TED JOHNS
### CHARLES LEATHERBARROW

Chartered Institute of Personnel and Development

Published by the Chartered Institute of Personnel and Development,
CIPD House, Camp Road, London, SW19 4UX

First published 2005

Design and typesetting by Curran Publishing Services, Norwich
Printed in Great Britain by The Cromwell Press, Trowbridge, Wiltshire

British Library Cataloguing in Publication Data
A catalogue record of this revision guide is available from the
British Library

ISBN 1 84398 084 3

Chartered Institute of Personnel and Development, CIPD House,
Camp Road, London, SW19 4UX
Tel: 020 8971 9000      Fax: 020 8263 3333
Email: cipd@cipd.co.uk      Website: www.cipd.co.uk
Incorporated by Royal Charter. Registered Charity No. 1079797

# CONTENTS

# FIGURES

# ABOUT THIS BOOK

This *People resourcing* revision guide is designed to supplement the core text for the 'People Resourcing' elective of the CIPD's Professional Development Scheme (PDS) which ultimately leads to Chartered Membership of the Institute. The core text is Stephen Taylor's *People resourcing* (2002, CIPD Publications) and both publications can be purchased through the CIPD's suppliers at a discounted price for CIPD members.

The *People resourcing* revision guide is one of a series designed to help candidates prepare for the Institute's professional examinations.

## What is in this guide?

Chapter 1 addresses the Professional Standards for People Resourcing. The standards are presented in full in Appendix 1. Chapter 1 attempts to translate and interpret the standards in terms of their meaning for HR practitioners in their everyday work. The chapter also gives an indication of how the standards are interpreted by the People Resourcing chief examiner, and how they influence the types of question posed in examinations.

Chapter 2 concerns itself with preparation for examinations. If you have already read one of the sister revision guides which covers the other electives or core programmes of study, you will find that some, although not all, of the material presented here is of a similar nature.

Chapter 3 contains the chief examiner's insights, and is a must if you are preparing for the next suite of examinations. Here the chief examiner dissects the previous November and May's diet of the People Resourcing examination: the intent of the questions, how they were answered, the strengths and weaknesses overall of the students who sat the papers.

Chapter 4 provides a detailed analysis and model responses to previous examination papers. From the 2004 examination we have included some responses from candidates' actual papers. These responses have been analysed for their strengths and weaknesses with a view to giving some insight into the methodology, the approach, to tackling a question.

The References section has been expanded and includes a range of relevant texts, reports and web addresses, supplemented by comments about their usefulness in the context of People Resourcing.

This book has been jointly written by Dr Ted Johns, the Chief Examiner for People Resourcing, and Charles Leatherbarrow. Dr Johns was responsible for contributing the Preface and Chapters 1 and 2, Charles Leatherbarrow for the remainder of the book.

Charles Leatherbarrow
Staffordshire University
July 2004

# PREFACE

## The thinking performer in a contributor culture

In selecting what to write for the preface I have chosen to address the philosophy that underpins the design and structure of the People Resourcing elective. You may have already come across the now fashionable aphorism, 'select for attitude and train for skill', which is meant to convey the idea that if an organisation needs its employees to behave and think in particular ways (for example, be enthusiastic towards customers), it is a lot easier to achieve that outcome if it recruits people with appropriate attitudes in the first place. It is certainly much harder to try to inculcate people with positive customer-facing attitudes after they have already joined, as many organisations have found when they have tried to change their culture when coping with a new, competitive environment. After all, people with the right attitudes can always be trained to produce the necessary skills and knowledge.

The same applies to budding HR professionals: namely, that the right attitude to begin with is more important than the straightforward possession of knowledge. So when you embark on your CIPD studies, and begin to address the obligations of the Professional Development Scheme, it is vital that, first, you understand what attitudes will be expected of you as you demonstrate your competencies, and second, you also understand what actions on your part – in the examinations, in the assignments, in your CPD activities and in your everyday conduct – will enable you to exhibit those attitudes in a thoroughly convincing fashion.

Simply by choosing to read this revision guide you have taken a significant step towards your final success not only in this subject, People Resourcing, but also in the CIPD's Professional Development Scheme as a whole. This is because my remarks will focus on the concept of the 'thinking performer' as far as its relevance to the whole of the CIPD's professional standards is concerned, and will show what it means to be a thinking performer and how you can translate the philosophy and attitudes behind the thinking performer concept into your examination performance, your assignments, and of course most importantly of all, into your day-to-day approach to your professional activities at work.

It is a truism to claim that we live in turbulent, fast-moving times (although some organisations are more turbulent and fast-moving than others). Now, as I write, the times are dangerous as well.

The evidence is in front of our eyes: war, the threat and reality of 'regime change' in both countries and companies, warnings about terrorism, and McDonald's recording its first losses for over 30 years. Now, we are told, Ford and General Motors in the United States are developing bulletproof cars for sale to the general public. These vehicles will look the same as ordinary models, but they can withstand shots from a .44 calibre Magnum, they will have an airtight seal with an internal supply of oxygen in case of a chemical assault, and have plates of ballistic steel and a reinforced fuel tank.

More than ever, in the UK economy, we need thinking performers. Professor Michael Porter of Harvard Business School, reporting on the performance of the UK economy in early 2003, pointed out that it is vital for us to move from 'competing on relatively low costs of doing business', which by and large is what this country has done for many years, to 'competing on unique value and innovation'. Trying to be successful in any business arena purely on the basis of low costs is a strategy that is ultimately counter-productive, because there is always somebody who can cut costs faster (for example, by moving production to eastern Europe or customer service operations to India), and there is always a point beyond which cost-cutting cannot be undertaken without serious harm to product quality and service delivery. Performing on the basis of cost, moreover, does not require people to be thinking performers: quite the contrary, it requires individuals to conform to the dictates of a predetermined process, it presupposes strict routines, and it seeks where possible to eliminate human beings altogether. Once organisations and economies seek to compete down the route of 'unique value and innovation', in Porter's phrase, things have to change as far as people management and people leadership are concerned.

Searching out 'unique value and innovation' depends on ideas, and ideas only come from people who are motivated, optimistic, resourceful and enthusiastic, who are prepared to use their initiative in furtherance of the organisation's vision, goals and objectives, and who are encouraged to go beyond the constraints of their job descriptions in order to 'think outside the box'.

The thinking performer, however, can only flourish in what I call a 'contributor culture'. A contributor culture looks the same as an ordinary organisation, at least to the casual observer, but like the new bulletproof cars from Ford and General Motors, it has some special features. The contributor culture has its own internal oxygen supply (committed, enthusiastic thinking performers), a reinforced fuel tank (committed, enthusiastic customers), and plates of ballistic steel (a 'big idea').

Armed with these defences, a contributor culture can withstand anything the competition can throw at it. Even better, it can withstand anything the world can throw at it. In a feature about 'Business in bad times' (5 April 2003), *The Economist* said that one of the things successful companies do when business is tough is 'to listen harder to their customers ... Customers are likely to be going through hard times too, and they may well show their appreciation of special consideration with more than a smile.' Being a contributor culture at moments like this represents an asset of almost measureless value.

So what is a contributor culture all about? More specifically, how does it relate to the CIPD's vision of the thinking performer?

Any organisation should expect its people to do what they are paid to do. This is the nub of the problem. Too many organisations (even in this age of so-called 'lean and mean' performance) do not expect all that much. For many, absence 'control' consists of paying people a bonus simply for turning up. Incompetence and mediocrity, once permitted, can become endemic; managers administer, control and constrain, but cannot lead; jobs are specified in terms of tasks to be performed, not accountabilities to be achieved.

In the best-performing organisations, by contrast, people are valued principally for their outputs – for their contribution. What these contributor culture organisations have are people who:

- will go the extra mile, demonstrating 'organisational citizenship' and 'discretionary' behaviour through their flexibility, their willingness to go beyond their job description, and indeed their view that the job description represents a baseline for personal development rather than a ceiling for individual effort

- will 'add value', making a difference through active participation in continuous improvement programmes, through their awareness of the 'big picture', and their readiness to ask awkward questions like 'Why do we ...?' and 'Why don't we ...?'.

These are the kinds of people that the CIPD celebrates in its portrayal of the thinking performer as the central plank in the Professional Development Scheme platform.

People in organisations are expected to be both efficient and effective. Being efficient is about doing things right – obeying the rules, enforcing procedures, complying with the law, implementing standardised processes, and mouthing the words in the corporate script. Being effective, by contrast, is about doing the right things – delivering results that make a difference, adding value through incremental improvement, or even initiating a wholly transformational change.

Many companies measure the efficiency of their staff in the mistaken belief that in doing so they are also measuring effectiveness. Even now there are large numbers of customer-contact people in call centres who are incentivised by the need to achieve, say, a throughput of 40 phone calls per hour, and who are penalised if their performance falls below this magic figure. Yet call duration is (for the most part) not what matters to the customer. And is it not the case that the customer's needs, and the customer's experience, should drive what gets measured and therefore what gets done? What seems to happen in reality is that faced with the awkward dilemma of trying to measure the customer experience, managers will concentrate instead on measuring something that is easily measurable (call duration) in the – largely forlorn – hope that one metric (call duration) is correlated with another (customer satisfaction).

Thinking performers are people who do things right and do the right things. Further, they understand that if there is a conflict between the two, then doing the right thing (for instance, sending the customer away satisfied) may justifiably take precedence over doing things right (for example, sticking to the strict letter of the law with regard to acceptance of returned goods). Above all, thinking performers are contributors:

- They perform in the sense that they deliver the day-to-day operational results expected from them.

- They 'add value' by reflecting about what is done and how it is done. For a thinking performer, it is not enough to be told that something 'has always been done that way'.

- They are curious about and alert to the outside world, aware of ideas being developed and tried out in other organisations. For a thinking performer, what matters is whether it works, not whether it appears in a textbook.

- They seek to support the 'big idea' and the 'big picture' for their organisation. Their perspective is generous, not mean, and their horizons are wide, not narrow.

- They accept continuous learning as a regular, unsurprising expectation associated with their jobs and with their professional obligations within the CIPD.

For you to succeed in your studies and in the assessment systems associated with the CIPD's Professional Development Scheme, assimilation of a thinking performer mentality is crucial. It may not be easy for you, especially if you are employed in an organisation that does not itself display a culture favourable to thinking performer attitudes, but you must remember that the aim of the Professional Development Scheme is not primarily to train you to perform your current role for your existing employer more efficiently, but rather to prepare you for a multi-faceted future within the personnel/HR profession.

Dr Ted Johns
Chief Examiner, People Resourcing

# SECTION I

CIPD PROFESSIONAL STANDARDS

# 1 CIPD PROFESSIONAL STANDARDS

## Introduction

To be able to function as a People Resourcing (PR) professional it is clear that the individual must also have a detailed understanding of the business in which he or she works and also the context in which it operates, that is, the social, political (legislative) and technological environments which impact upon what business does and how it can do it. In addition, there is a need to systematically consider how we, as PR professionals, ply our trade. The CIPD standards are designed to guide our thinking and actions with respect to the processes for which we are responsible.

The purpose of this chapter is to review the PR Generalist Standards in context of the overall objectives of the CIPD thrust for development of a value-added contribution to business outcomes, and specifically with reference to the assessment of these standards. The standards are presented in headings below, and in detail in Appendix 1 of this revision guide.

The recommended text for this elective is Stephen Taylor's *People resourcing* (2002). Candidates working towards the examination can also find suggested further reading on the CIPD's website by going to the home page and following the drop-down menus as detailed below:

Site map —> Learner and tutor resources (click 'Resources for students'.) —> Student recommended reading list

This site provides the complete reading list to support all standards. The author has indicated further reading in the Bibliography. The twice-monthly house journal of the Institute, *People Management*, is also vital reading.

Candidates will be expected to think through examination questions and apply good practice in making decisions and recommendations for action based upon informed opinion. This implies that, when preparing for the examination, candidates need to commit to memory examples of good practice, perhaps from *People Management*, Taylor's *People resourcing* or other recognised sources. Although candidates are not expected to quote verbatim research outcomes, they are expected to be aware of research and the commentators who have contributed to the field of research and its outcomes. For example, when discussing the reliability of selection techniques, candidates would be expected to give the relative reliabilities of the methodologies (structured interview, assessment centre and so on), and indicate the source (for example, Anderson and Shackleton, or Smith *et al*).

## The People Resourcing Standards

The CIPD standards are presented under the following headings:

- Purpose
- Performance indicators
    - Operational indicators
    - Knowledge indicators
- Indicative content.

### Purpose

This section, as well as contextualising the focus of the PR process, gives a clear direction for what human resources professionals should be trying to achieve in their roles as business partners.

There has to be a marriage between operational transactional work and its outcomes, and the added-value element which can only be delivered by the thoughtful application of the knowledge and skills associated with the PR role.

Those entering the profession need both to focus on the 'here and now' and to develop their understanding of the strategic way PR impacts upon the business.

### Performance indicators

The *performance indicators* are considered in terms of what the HR practitioner must be able to do, and these are expressed as *operational indicators*. The aspects the practitioner must be able to understand and explain are expressed as *knowledge indicators*.

The *operational indicators* cannot be assessed in the exam room because they are associated with the actual application of knowledge and skills in the workplace, and so can only be assessed 'on the job'.

### Indicative content

The broad-brush *operational* and *knowledge indicators* are given detailed meaning by the *indicative content,* of which there are 10 sections:

1. PR in context.

2. The strategic significance of PR.

3. Approaches to PR.

4. HR planning.

5. Recruitment and selection.

6. People management.

7. Special-case scenarios.

8. Support tools for effective PR.

9. Compliance and ethicality in PR.

10. PR: the future.

## Understanding the performance indicators

The development of the performance indicators is predicated upon developing staff who have the ability and motivation to meet the demands of the CIPD's concept of the thinking performer, which implies both personal challenge and reflection on how to:

- deliver better standards

- do things quicker and smarter

- reduce the costs of PR activities

    – all while maintaining legal and regulatory compliance.

Accepting that 'I cannot make an impact in my organisation because I am not senior enough' is now thinking the unacceptable. We all have a contribution to make, and our ability to think and to demonstrate this quality will, given time, shake the foundations of the most backward-thinking organisations. Business, government, local government and other agencies cannot afford not to fully employ all their talent at all levels.

Performance Indicators 1 and 2 have many things in common. They are about enhancing policies, processes and procedures. Individually we can continually challenge ourselves and test whether or not there is room for improvement. We should also consider the paradigms that corporately cause our organisation, and other organisations, to reflect, and to test what they and we do to challenge the status quo.

You should maintain a 'knitting vigilance' by monitoring *People Management*, *The Times* and similar quality broadsheets. The core text and other recommended texts all contribute to informing opinion. 'Being aware of and appraised of issues' is part of the approach to business improvement. To complete the process there must be reflection, recommendation, debate and then action. Consider, for example, the whole paradigm of resourcing. Although the contingency approach to PR has been around since the 1950s, it had largely lain fallow until recently, when there has been a resurgence of interest. Academically, the contingency approach considers the best fit between process and the nature of the business. Large firms typically have processes in place which reflect the need for uniformity of action, perhaps more bureaucracy, whereas the smaller firm, such as an advertising company, might see its differentiating characteristic in terms both of how it sells itself to customers, and how it attracts and retains staff, as 'being different': the need to have well-tried policies and procedures is not seen as fitting with the company culture (Taylor 2002, p14). The essence of preparation, therefore, is to review and identify issues, and to reflect on them, which should ultimately lead to recommendations for action, or perhaps inaction. In the case quoted, the fact that the PR professional is aware of the trends should at least stimulate thought about whether or not the paradigm is relevant to his or her business.

## 1. Make constructive contributions to the development or enhancement of PR policies

Policies and procedures are specific to a subject area of the PR process but generic in terms of how we handle, create, review and revise them. No single chapter of Taylor's core text (*People resourcing*) deals specifically with how policies should be handled. However, within each chapter Taylor deals with good, bad and value-added practice. The clues about what we should be doing are there. The issue, of course, is what are we doing about it? Is the good, and especially value-added, practice included within the policies with which we work on a day-to-day basis?

The changing world in which we live, and the technological advances in the integration of production methods and communications systems, impact on the way business operates within the United Kingdom and across borders. This when coupled with political changes such as the fall of the Iron Curtain, the dropping of trade barriers with China, its accession to the World Trade Organisation and the 'aggrandisement' of the European Union, have all increased the pace of change in how we work and the nature of the work. The fundamental relationship between employer and employee has changed, and the increasing influences of stakeholder interest are all reflected in the world in which we work.

We are in a post-modern society (Huczynski and Buchanan 2001, p58) where not only the technologies have changed but also societal and individual values.

Policies are in effect a plan of action, which reflect the deliberations of and also capture the wisdom of those competent to make value judgements on sets of circumstances. The net result is a set of recommended actions in response to a set of circumstances. Circumstances, however, change very quickly. Changes are brought about by macro and micro reasons, for example, the impact of the destruction of the World Trade Centre in New York in 2001 because of its resulting impact upon the airline and tourism business and the reluctance of people to fly was immense. Micro changes caused by local competition in the labour market can all have a significant effect upon PR.

Processes need to be in place to review the relevance and efficacy of PR policies. It is about added value. Outdated and outmoded policies may be at best value-neutral, and at worse cause frustration and fail to facilitate the business process.

The challenge has to be twofold. On the one hand there is a continuous requirement to challenge the norm, and to question and test what is in place against some form of yardstick. On the other hand there has to be a pragmatism that reflects the limitations that are put on business processes because of resource constraints (staffing level, cash or cash flow). It is important to understand these factors and to be able to demonstrate the pragmatism of decision-making.

To give an example, the author was working in an overseas joint venture (JV) operation drilling for hydrocarbons in the North Caspian Sea. At one stage of the venture there was a clear requirement for extra competent staff, to meet adequately both the requirements of the drilling operation and the not insubstantial reporting requirements of the JV shareholders. However, a business decision was taken to limit further recruitment because the well that was being drilled was a 'wildcat' (first well) in a 'prospect' that was still being appraised. Oil and gas had not yet been found, and it was not yet clear that the well, and thus the prospect, was going to produce hydrocarbons in economic quantities. Until this became clearer, recruitment was restricted to the replacement of key staff, people lost through attrition. Clearly this was a painful decision but it was taken because of ethical and also practical considerations. The decision was ethical in the sense that the company wished to minimise the number of staff it might have to make redundant should the well not detect and produce hydrocarbons in commercial quantities, and it was practical because only poor-quality individuals were likely to apply for positions in a company with a possible limited lifespan. For management the issue was to prepare for two scenarios:

1.  A 'dry' well and thus staff would have to be made redundant.

2.  A successful appraisal of the prospect and an immediate expansion of the project.

Scenario 1 infers a progressive scaling-down of operations and all that implies. Scenario 2 infers that the whole scale of the business changes, from a one-well JV operation to a multi-billion-dollar exploration and production programme, which was the case. This sea change in activity would have to be reflected in new ways of doing business, new structures, strategies, policies and so on. Clearly time and effort was spent planning for this eventuality. In the meantime the policy was communicated to staff as part of the open policy of sharing information. (See Figure 1.)

**Figure 1** Delivering business objectives in the context of resource constraints

Source: Taylor (2002)

### *Reflecting upon the business practice of PR and sharing learning*

To come back to the issues at hand, how can practitioners reflect on this type of issue in their work and in their professional studies and revision?

1.  First, this can be achieved by reflecting upon your own business practice. How do you maintain a currency of policies and procedures within your work? Are they live working documents that truly reflect the needs of the business?

    –   How are they audited?

    –   What triggers cause (have caused) a revision of their relevance and effectiveness?

    –   What are the strengths and weaknesses in current processes?

2.  Second, what is good practice? In his core text *People resourcing*, Taylor (2002, ch15) gives some examples of how we can measure what we do in this respect in demonstrating added value. He offers a number of ways in which this can be done. By measuring

effectiveness of the PR activities we can then debate and discuss what is going right, what is going wrong and therefore what should be changed.

3.  Third, it can be achieved by monitoring articles in *People Management* and identifying good practice, and noting and committing to memory some relevant studies.

4.  Fourth, and perhaps the most powerful, is the learning that candidates can gain by sharing information. Working as a member of a team is better than the individual working alone. The PR examination is non-competitive, so groups who are following the programme of study can work effectively together and support each other's learning by sharing good practice.

One of the most effective ways in which the course leader/learning facilitator can help is by structuring classes so that the learning process becomes a shared event. The aim is to create an environment where students are able to access the curriculum (performance indicators, knowledge indicators and indicative content) by bringing to the class their own experiences through tutorials and effectively 'peer teaching'. In this way all can share in good, and sometimes reflect upon bad, practice.

There are of course practical, legal and ethical issues associated with this process. From a practical standpoint the course leader has to facilitate the process by setting the scene and making time for presentation and subsequent discussion. Ethically some of the issues discussed may involve practices and perhaps outcomes relevant to individuals and individual firms, governmental organisations and so on, so there has to be a shared understanding that discussion and debate is confidential within the confines of the classroom. Individual students have to be relied upon to sanitise presentations so as not to break confidences with clients or customer groups, or to contravene the Data Protection Act.

## 2. Evaluate existing PR processes, systems and procedures, and propose cost-effective improvements

This performance indicator is woven throughout all the major activities within the scope of PR. There is a need to manage an organisation, and the quality of the administration that supports the management activity can significantly impact upon the bottom line. Taylor (2002, p7) quotes the following activities that can significantly impact upon the business if the supporting procedures are not cost-effective:

- human resource planning

- job analysis

- developing competency frameworks

- drawing up job descriptions, person specifications and account-ability profiles.

Pragmatically the individual cannot do everything, so there must be processes and systems in place which generate challenge, and perhaps cause a review of current practice. These could range from internal or external audits of sections of the business to including the responsibility for system reviews as a performance objective for the coming year.

In preparing for examinations the student is advised to follow the practice described above for Performance Indicator 1. What processes and systems have been introduced that deliver what the customer wants quicker or cheaper, or perhaps offer more choice and flexibility? Using the processes of sharing information (see above, 'Reflecting upon the business practice of PR'), students are encouraged to work together, to share good practice, to track events in *People Management* and to discuss and debate issues during class. Clearly students need to be proactive in identifying and recording events that reflect this type of change. To quote in part from Taylor (2002, pxv), this entails:

- keeping in touch with the outside world, not just in the sector where you are working, in order to pick up ideas of performance improvement

- sustaining an open-minded attitude to innovation, so that ideas are not merely or automatically rejected … to focus on the constructive application of ideas

- understanding your organisation's strategic direction, goals and objectives, plus their role in contributing to the attainment of these purposes

- networking with customers, both internal and external, in order to keep in touch with the business, seek out feedback and learn lessons from it

- proactively developing (or contributing to the development of) service innovations that yield customer advantage

- acknowledging that compliance is not a sufficient yardstick for measuring the effectiveness of the personnel/HR function and that corporate contribution is a more relevant indicator.

### 3. Optimise the available tools and techniques in the field of IT (including the Internet) for all aspects of PR

Item 8 of the indicative content covers this performance indicator. Globalisation trends and advances in information technology are driving today's business. Consider this comment made in 2000 by Goran Lindahl, then chief executive officer of ABB (quoted in Joynt and Morton 2000, p61):

> If talent is one side of the global competitive equation, information systems/technology (IS/IT) is the other ... the two areas which will have the highest impact on our operations for the next five years are human resources (HR) and information technology (IT).

Knowledge Indicator 8(1) covers the application of IT to the PR processes. Indicator 8(2) is about where to obtain information about IT systems, benchmarking and so on.

Of interest in the context of this book is the application of IT (e-HR) to the PR business processes. We can think of this in two ways:

1. The use of IT (e-HR) systems in support of internal HR processes.

2. The introduction and impact of IT (e-HR) systems to replace, or to operate in parallel with, traditional PR processes that interface with the outside world (recruitment, selection, information sources and so on).

### Focusing on item 1

The implications for study involve understanding how IT systems are employed and can replace traditional paper-based systems. The bigger question is what is, and possibly could be, their impact on PR practice and the way HR professionals go about their work? This is not limited to how they can use IT (e-HR) and decide what is best practice, but involves considering the wider implications for the way HR supports the business now that knowledge and information can be distributed in such a readily accessible (potentially 24 hours a day, seven days a week) and interactive form. Already global business is applying this technology in its PR activities and assessing further new ways to best use this increasingly reliable and flexible technology (Taylor 2002, pp23–27).

### Focusing on item 2

In some ways, this is more straightforward because it deals with the practice of using IT systems to replace traditional practices used in recruitment, selection and so on. The innovative ideas that web-based technology offers in terms of, for example, selection testing cannot be ignored. The PR practitioner is expected to know where IT systems are used and their advantages and disadvantages. This is a moving target, so relying on textbook information alone to maintain a currency of practice and awareness is insufficient.

Embracing all practice which involves IT systems are the compliance requirements of the Data Protection Act (DPA). The HR professional is expected to know the fundamental requirements of the Act, and how to apply good practice so as to ensure regulatory compliance.

### 4. Assist with the design, development, implementation and review of PR methods to resolve specific corporate scenarios

Representative samples of the above are given as: geographical relocation, new business development, management of an acquisition, corporate restructuring, graduate/expatriate appointments, delayering, devolution, decentralisation, retrenchment, and using an outsourcing partner such a recruitment agency.

This performance indicator is included in recognition of the fact that the HR professional is likely to be impacted upon, at some time in his or her career, by some big-picture activities. He or she should therefore be prepared to tackle the fallout from decisions to embark upon one or more of the above major scenarios, and be able to guide the management response in HR issues.

Clearly the student cannot and will not be able to consider every possible contingency, and successively reflect and research responses for each event. The student can, though, consider some of the scenarios, research good practice, and transfer relevant practice and processes in response to the unknown. This is where the *thinking performer* and all that this concept represents kicks in. It is about transferring knowledge and relevant practice, and applying intelligence to solving related problems – 'Intelligence is what you do when you don't know what to do' (Jean Piaget).

Candidates are expected to be able to apply themselves to the practical aspects of, for example, a downsizing exercise. What is good practice, what are the legal requirements in terms of consultation and preparation of redundancy terms, offers of alternative work and so on? Hand in glove with these process-driven activities there are the issues that arise when deciding how to identify outplacement contractors. Candidates need to be aware of applicable and good practice in this type of field. However, once they have worked through an example, and read through and explored case studies in class, the concept is readily transferable to other unrelated but similar scenarios.

## 5. Undertake the full range of day-to-day functions for which the PR professional generally is accountable

The specific range of functions for which any HR professional is accountable depends on the industry sector in which he or she operates, but there are some core functions for which all PR professionals are accountable:

- recruitment

- performance

- reward

- retention

- release.

This is the 'knitting' of our business. These are the areas where there is a need to be aware of innovative practices which save time and effort and give service options, and also to demonstrate competence in their selection and application.

Section 5 of the indicative content details what this means in respect of the recruitment and selection activities; however, the analysis can be applied to each of the five core activities above, and so gives guidance on how you should approach preparing for the examination:

- *the background*: criteria for administration, considerations of alternative process options

- *the processes*: principal methods, features, benefits and disadvantages

- *measurement of effectiveness*: techniques for monitoring outcomes, currency and relevance of processes, compliance and continuous improvement.

In essence this is the detail of how the PR professional goes about his or her business. Candidates will be expected to know the key processes together with applicable theory and background, and should commit to memory examples of good or innovative practice, and appreciate the relative advantages and disadvantages of the competing processes. For example Torrington *et al* (2002, pp174–187) offer an excellent window on recruitment issues, covering in a succinct manner the options and their relative merits. The increasing focus is on informed opinion, so candidates should be able to offer supporting theoretical evidence with some reference sources.

## 6. Contribute to human resource plans that relate to and achieve business/corporate goals

Sections 1 and 4 of the indicative content detail, in the main, the coverage of this performance indicator. Traditionally HR planning has been associated with large corporate enterprises and public sector organisations, and the 'hard' statistical analysis of HR data. This essentially was the process of demand forecasting – staff retiring, staff under development and training, numbers to be recruited. A typical example of this is the macro planning for teacher recruitment and training, based on demographic trends and the need to provide extra social facilities as urban populations change. There is still a need for this type of analysis, but the context of HR planning has changed.

Taylor (2002, p70) quoting Mintzberg (1994), puts the case *against* HR planning. However, candidates should be aware that there are equally powerful cases *for* HR planning (Taylor 2002, p73).

Planning in the context of PR covers a wide scope. There is a need to focus outward, to understand the external environment and the context in which business operates. This would include analysis of socio-demographic trends, the political arena and social trends: for example, the increasing demand for a recognition of the work/life balance and how this type of social change is being reflected in the introduction of 'family-friendly' legislation.

There is also a requirement for an inward focus, to ascertain the current status of the business and trends of staffing utilisation over time. To collate this data is no good unless it is analysed and interpreted to assess what it means for the business in terms of PR, and then put to some practical use – perhaps to inform managers that they have a problem in staff turnover. The capacity to identify the specific department where this is occurring adds value by providing information, not speculation. Gone are the days when personnel crunched the weekly data taken from time cards. Using modern, and relatively inexpensive, management information systems, the tracking of key administrative information like staff turnover and absence is well within the scope of the smallest business. When considering the broader, longer-term perspective, data can be used to inform decisions on recruitment, training and development, staff cost forecasting, redundancy, collective bargaining and office accommodation (Taylor 2002, p76).

When considering the impact of different business scenarios on the requirement for staff, the process of 'contingency planning' (Taylor 2002, p79–80) better informs all aspects of the PR process, from succession and skills planning through to recruitment and release of staff.

### Measuring today to plan for tomorrow

Candidates need to get to grips with the basics of the hard side of HR planning:

- Indices and how they are used:

- Labour Turnover Index
- Stability Index
- profitability or cost per employee.

(These indices can be applied to all or parts of the business.)

- Methods of trend analysis:
  - cohort analysis
  - census method
  - retention profiles.

With this type of information, better decisions can be made in support of future business plans. They also enable interpretation, with some objectivity, of what is happening, and has happened over time, with respect to employee stability/turnover.

In addition to the above factors, which can be used to inform the effectiveness of current activities on a day-to-day level, there is a need, at a higher level of practice, to analyse the alignment or 'fit' of HR strategies with the overarching business strategy and objectives. If business objectives seek to include the development of teamwork and knowledge management, the reward strategy must reflect these requirements by rewarding effective teams, and practices that encourage the dissemination of knowledge throughout the business. There is a need to analyse the 'fit' of HR policies, practices and strategies to ensure that they are holistic and make a coherent whole.

Leading and supporting 'change management' requires a thorough understanding of how the business works. This means not only the interlinking structures and communication links, but also how politics and the use of power bring about both desirable and undesirable outcomes. Although it is considered by many that political behaviour can be damaging to a business, Senior (2002, p174), recognises that it is a fact of life, a given, that 'power politics' will be a game played by some, if not all, of those involved. Planning is the first step to change, and the reality is that some form of political behaviour will manifest itself during the change process. The HR practitioner should be aware of how power and politics play their part in bringing about change.

### Contribution to business planning

Once again the focus is on adding value. Being prepared to contribute to business planning ensures HR, and in particular the PR practitioner, a place at the table where strategic decisions are made.

We saw above how by understanding what is happening in the business by measurement of current activity, the *inward focus* enables the practitioner to make informed decisions on the progress of activities, efficiency and effectiveness. He or she can thus contribute to problem-solving and the development of business plans, as well as the strategies to deliver the plans.

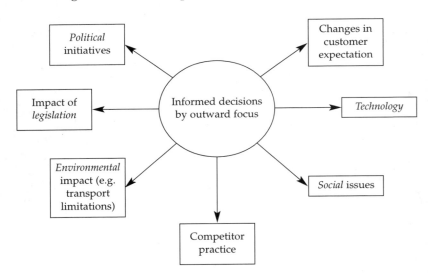

**Figure 2** Contribution to business planning by *outward focusing*

Figure 2 represents what would, in traditional change management, constitute a PESTL analysis (political, economic, social, technological, legal) of the business environment (refer to Senior (2002, pp15–16), for a full discussion on the PESTL or PETS analysis. However, it is a 'PESTL analysis Plus' because the outward reflection and analysis considers further influencing factors which impinge on business planning.

## *Softer planning issues*

### *Reflection*

Performance Indicator 6 is a statement of the 'HR territory' or HRM business model, which was first presented by Beer and Spector in 1984 and which became known as the 'Harvard model' of HRM. Later modifications were made which better reflect the non-North American socio-political and business environment: for example, one of the first approaches to HRM in the UK was articulated by David Guest who developed a number of propositions which could be tested. As Beardwell and Holden, 2001, pp19–21 point out it is the combination of these propositions of Strategic Integration; High Commitment; High Quality and Flexibility which lead to more effective organisations. Candidates should be aware of these models and their seminal influence on the development of HRM.

## 7. Critically evaluate PR systems and new approaches or methodologies

From a practitioner's viewpoint the annual budget exercise is enough to cause a flurry of activity and a proportional amount of navel gazing about what the HR function will be involved with in the forthcoming year. There is a requirement to answer three very fundamental questions:

1.  What PR activities will the (HR) function be involved with in the forthcoming year?

2.  What will they cost (as activities)?

3.  What will be the implications for (HR) staffing?

Taylor (2002, ch15) deals with the costing of activities; he calls this chapter 'Demonstrating added value'. It is a good place to start thinking about the costing processes, if for no other reason than because they form part of the annual planning cycle. Once it is known what activities will be entered into during the next planning period (which is all linked into the overall business plan and strategies), and what it costs to perform these activities (rituals?), we can then begin to understand where significant cost centres lie, and so be in a position to decide to do something about costing and planning.

As an example, Taylor (2002, p385) conducts a cost–benefit analysis in which he analyses a series of work experience programmes for school leavers and then compares the outcome of this exercise, in terms of numbers recruited as a direct outcome of the experience, with the traditional cost of recruitment via newspaper advertising. This type of cost–benefit analysis, although simplistic in nature, is a very powerful tool for the 'legitimisation' of decisions made or yet to be made.

The above analysis applies quantitative measures to the evaluation process, but candidates must also consider that decisions are not always so simple, and decisions based on a mix of quantitative and qualitative measures are generally the norm. Depending upon circumstance, issues such as reputation are as important as the saving of a few thousand pounds.

Candidates in the context of this Performance Indicator are expected to be able to break activities down into their cost elements (as described above) and to apply average rates for contractors, room rental and so on. This in turn implies that candidates are aware of going rates for contractors, hourly or day rates for administration work, and so on. So often, when asked to cost an activity, candidates omit the administration costs. When they are asked why, the response more often than not is along the lines, 'The administrator is already in place so there are no cost implications.' This infers that there is no 'on cost' to the business for this activity. This is a fallacious argument because, in reality, administration costs should be considered as 'opportunity costs'.

### PR: the future

Previous examination questions have specifically tested candidates' awareness of the wider and longer-term picture, which may be coloured by social or legislative events. The indicative content (No 10) gives some examples of issues that candidates should be aware of, and for which they should above all have considered what impact they might have on their business, business sector and thus PR processes.

As a candidate and PR professional, how do you address this requirement? Is it asking too much? The simple answer to the second question is no, it is not asking too much. You would be quite upset if you visited a doctor or a primary care practitioner and found that he or she was using practice and theory that was outdated, and was not aware of current thinking and trends on medicine. By a similar token you cannot expect to maintain the respect of those you work for, your peers and those who work for the PR profession, if as a PR professional you are not maintaining a currency of practice and awareness of the wider present and future issues that might have an impact on the way business functions.

The indicative content mentions:

1. Debates over the future of work and employment, especially in view of continuing technological change, globalisation, and the growth of e-commerce (and eHR – *author's addition*).

2. The dilemma of seeking to reconcile the interests and preferences of individual employees with the requirements and expectations of organisations.

3. New thinking and research on topics relevant to PR such as:

   – matching personality types or learning styles with specific occupational roles

   – the effectiveness of psychometric tests

   – emotional intelligence

   – knowledge management.

4. Actual and potential developments in employment legislation and other compliance arenas.

How does one prepare for this in the context of the PR examination? There is no 'cure all' response to this question, say by homing in on key topics. It is, though, possible to consider the process offered and discussed in Performance Indicator no 1 not only as good examination preparation, but as one that can inform continued professional development.

## 8. Co-operate positively with executive/managerial stakeholders – 'customers' in the design and implementation of resourcing processes

This performance indicator reinforces two roles:

1.  That the PR professional is responsible for a key function which demonstrably impacts upon the bottom line. The role, by definition, carries a managerial weight and therefore it is incumbent upon PR managers/business partners to communicate effectively on issues, plans, strategies, processes and policies to relevant stakeholders.

2.  That the PR professional is at the same time performing as a service provider, and therefore there is a notion of accountability to those for whom that service is provided.

Item 2.2 of the indicative content identifies the stakeholders, and the need to develop working relationships with those involved:

- managers with devolved accountabilities for PR

- outsourced contractors

- recruitment agencies and executive search consultants, outplacement agencies and so on.

### 9. Advocate and ensure compliance with all appropriate ethical and legal obligations associated with PR

The details of the requirements of this performance indicator are provided in Section 9 of the indicative content.

### Comments on legislation

Candidates are expected to know and understand key legislation, and above all how it is applied to the PR process; this is the added value that the PR professional brings to the table.

This includes legislation generated both in the United Kingdom and from the European Union. Much legislation surrounds issues of discrimination, whether direct or indirect. Below is a list of areas of legislation of which the PR professional should have a working knowledge:

- human rights legislation

- disability discrimination

- equal opportunities

- race relations

- data protection
- the employment relationship (recruitment, selection, contracts of employment, discipline, grievance, dismissal issues, and so on)
- health and safety.

### Ethical and professional considerations

Ethical considerations also play a significant part in today's business practice. Friedman (1963), quoted in Torrington *et al* (2002, p25), posits that business should focus on 'doing business' within the 'rules of the game' and the law, and it is not the responsibility of the manager to engage in promoting social and therefore ethical issues.

This is not the stance of the CIPD for two very good reasons. The first is the recognition that business does not operate in a vacuum, but in the world we live in, and in which we 'do business'. Business ethics should therefore reflect the higher values and norms of this society. It is about being a good citizen. This is not to imply that the HR practitioner takes an evangelistic stance and is a beacon of righteousness. Rather the stance has to be pragmatic, honest, and fair when choices have to be made. The second reason that good, fair, ethical practice cannot be ignored is quite simply a hard-headed business reason: to ignore it can impact negatively on business effectiveness and profitability. Stakeholders in the business, external and internal, consciously or subconsciously reflect upon business practices, and these have an influence when they make decisions about the company. A perception that employees are treated fairly reflects upon the ability to attract new employees. The perception that employees' contributions to debates and issues are considered and incorporated into corporate reflections, and so influence higher-level decision-making, impacts upon employee commitment. Recognising that diversity can positively lever business opportunities and that tribunals (for example dealing with equal opportunity issues) are costly, and at the same time impact upon business reputation, is a 'bottom line' issue which cannot be ignored. The notion of the 'critical success factor' is common in the language of today's business, but there is also a need to be aware (as the indicative content makes clear) of those issues that fit neatly under the heading of 'critical failure factor'.

None of the above should be taken to imply that HR practices should reflect a 'softness' in business practice. The HR manager, or in our case the PR business partner, has to be respected and valued for the contribution made to the decision-making process when dealing with his or her management colleagues. Candidates should be aware of examples of good practice, perhaps from *People Management* case studies, where business ethics has impacted positively or negatively on business outcomes.

### 10. Apply the principles and practice of continuing professional development (CPD) for their own personal development

Because this revision guide specifically focuses on preparing candidates for the CIPD examination in PR, the topic of CPD is not addressed in this text.

## Questions related to the performance standards

Question-spotting is not recommended, but theme-spotting is. What I mean by this relates to the awareness of PR candidates to the trends: for example topics that the government announces are to be covered in Green and White Papers, debates in the national press, and reports in our own professional house journal *People Management* which are clearly relevant in the context of today's business environment. These may be driven by advances in technology and/or changes in social trends, or perhaps national or European legislation, or new research on the employment relationship.

Let us consider how some of elements of the indicative content can be interpreted in the context of my comments above.

### (1) People resourcing in context, (4) Human resource planning (9) Compliance and ethical obligations in people resourcing

*Demographic trends and full employment*: during 2003 and 2004 there has been much debate in the press and professional journals about the impact of the UK's ageing population and the impact upon business in a time when the United Kingdom is experiencing full employment. PR candidates should be aware of both the overarching demographic trends and what it means for HR planning. The implications of the greying population have been discussed in *People Management*, and in articles in *The Times* (2004), and the *Sunday Times* (2004), to name but three, as well as on television and radio. If these trends are coupled with the current debate about the European legislation on age discrimination, which the United Kingdom is proposing to adopt in 2006, then the issues for HR advisors are significant and complex.

Candidates should be aware both of the wider issues, as presented above, and of how they impact upon the resourcing of employees, which of course is the focus of this guide. Analysis of the questions that can be teased from the above makes good material for tutorials, which in turn inform your professional practice and preparation for the examination.

Changes in the demographics in terms of an ageing population cause us to consider what the implications are for:

- The current pension legislation.

- The personal drivers of those over 60 years of age in terms of the balance between work and life and motivational influences. Are they the same for this cohort as for those of younger years? What is industry doing to respond to these workforce changes?

- Business: should the government adopt EU legislation on age discrimination? What are the current debates and who is participating in them?

Further impacting upon the above is the change to the size of the European Community as a further 10 countries joined in May 2004. From a resourcing perspective this opened up a whole new labour market for the UK employer. However, employing EU nationals raises a raft of issues, including the determination of the equivalence of qualifications, measurement of competency, proof of identity and therefore eligibility for work, and compliance with UK legislation in respect of the checks required on those who are applying to work with vulnerable members of our society.

The November 2003 and May 2004 diet of the PR examinations addressed some of the above issues.

### *(6) People management*

One clear area of the focus of our attention under this heading is initiatives on and research under the heading of 'people management' per se. Over the period 2003/2004 there have been a number of notable initiatives and developments in this area. Angela Baron, for example, has made a number of presentations on 'Measuring and managing human capital and people'. Not unexpectedly there has been significant interest and debate about the link between the 'bottom line' and the management of people. The latter also causes reflection on topics like knowledge management and emotional intelligence. The development of these themes can be observed through the relevant articles as they are published in *People Management*, and in research reports, especially those the CIPD has commissioned. Common sense says that we should use this information in our everyday business, and also our longer-term strategic thinking. It goes without saying that knowledge of the content of these documents should form part of the essential preparation for examinations. The list of CIPD research papers, Change Agendas and Guides in the Bibliography is not exhaustive, but it does give a focus for reflection and thus personal development.

As indicated, candidates are expected to know of the existence of these reports and their key findings. For example, in the May 2004 PR examination a Section B question explored the issues and relativities of staff turnover in different industry sectors. In consideration of staff turnover candidates would not be expected to quote 'line and verse' of the various turnover statistics for each of the industry sectors or occupations; they would, though, be expected to have a concept of what constitutes low and average turnover, and knowledge of those occupations and sectors that experience high turnover. With this information at hand candidates would then be able to interpret, analyse and so make value judgements in terms of the impact upon business outcomes. Candidates would be expected to have an understanding of the factors that impinge upon high turnover, and the options open to management to mitigate their impact.

### (9) Compliance and ethicality obligations in PR

Legislative compliance is the bread of the 'bread and butter' of the PR professional's work. Adding value counts for nothing if we do not get the basics correct. There have been many questions in past PR examinations on the care required during the recruitment and selection process to ensure that no discriminatory bias is shown to particular individuals or groups. The world of PR professionals is changing, though, because of:

- technological advances

- globalisation of industry

- the impact of an enlarged EU and the opportunities this brings for PR

- changes in legislation, driven by both the UK government and the EU.

In the context of these changes there have been a significant number of recent and well-published events, which have impacted upon how we conduct our business.

Considering one of these themes, technological advances, for example, in its base terms information technology allows us to readily interchange, store and access vast amounts of information on people from remote and distributed locations. Governing the use of data storage is the Data Protection Act (DPA). PR professionals should know and understand what this Act means to them, the opportunities it presents, and the restrictions it poses on data interchange and storage. As a result of the inquiry chaired by Sir Michael Bichard into the murder of Jessica Chapman and Holly Wells, a number of shortcomings were highlighted in the way various police authorities capture and hold data, and misunderstandings of the way the DPA can be applied.

The inquiry had as one of its terms of reference, 'to assess the effectiveness of the relevant intelligence-based record keeping, the vetting practices in those forces since 1995 ... and make recommendations as appropriate'. With the outcomes of the inquiry in mind (and recognising that many of us recruit staff to work with vulnerable members of our society), it is incumbent upon us to make the essential security checks. These give us the confidence that we are recruiting only those whose background is not blemished by behaviours that lead us to believe that the individual would pose a risk if employed in a capacity that gives access to those who need protection. Due diligence requires that the fundamentals are in place; references should be followed up and checks made on qualifications claimed. Professionally we should be aware of the agencies that can provide these essential checks, from the Criminal Records Bureau to those private organisations that can provide baseline checks on educational qualifications. The following is from the text of the Bichard inquiry (www.bichardinquiry.org.uk), and serves to highlight the need for due diligence. However, it recognises that even if all the checks had been correctly made, Ian Huntley would have still been recruited into the village college at Soham:

> There are, nonetheless, a number of aspects in Huntley's recruitment process which give rise to concern. In particular:
>
> 2.164.1 Soham Village College should not have accepted the 'open' references provided by Huntley, particularly in circumstances where it was clear that he had not previously held any post involving significant contact with children, and accordingly none of the references were directed to, or even considered, the issue of his suitability to work with children.
>
> 2.164.2 The interview process failed to identify either the employment history gaps or undisclosed employers in Huntley's application.
>
> 2.164.3 There was no reason why the police check process could not have been completed before Huntley started work at the school.
>
> 2.165 In my view, as Mr. Gilbert (*the headmaster of Soham Village College – author's clarification*) properly accepted during the course of giving evidence, it was a mistake on his part not to take up the references. It does not, of course, follow that if he had done so anything further would have been revealed. It also appears from the subsequent enquiries made by Cambridgeshire Constabulary that at least four of the references were authentic. However, the failure to follow up the references fell short of acceptable recruitment practice relating to people applying to work with children, and could in itself have had significant implications.

In considering globalisation and HR, *People Management*, the national press, television and radio have reported on the way a number of NHS trusts have taken advantage of the opportunities of recent relaxing of legislation to allow the recruitment of key workers from overseas into caring occupations, in areas the trusts have found it difficult to resource. This brings with it incumbent problems. Some of the problems are associated with selecting staff who have the appropriate attitudes and mindsets to cope with living in a foreign country, in this case the United Kingdom, for the duration of their contract. There still remains the requirement to ensure that those who apply are who they say they are, have bona fide qualifications, and can be trusted to work with the vulnerable.

The author has had first-hand experience of potential recruits presenting forged degrees and other qualifications from both UK and overseas institutions. In this respect, the added value is in knowing 'where to go' to determine the bona fide credentials of individuals (who they say they are) and the authenticity of documents (what they say they are). In this way the HR professional is both demonstrating professionalism by engaging in appropriate due diligence checks, and as indicated, adding value by facilitating innovative approaches to PR.

# SECTION 2

## HOW TO TACKLE REVISION
## AND THE EXAMINATION

# 2 REVISION AND EXAMINATION GUIDANCE

## Introduction

To begin with, you should understand clearly the underpinning philosophical attitudes and values that the chief examiner and his team bring to the process of assessing your examination script. These have been discussed and outlined in the preface to this revision guide, but they deserve to be re-emphasised here if only because they show that the criteria are not based on some whimsical preferences developed by the chief examiner, but are linked to the CIPD's strategic vision for itself (and for its members). They are reflected in all the electives for the Professional Development Scheme (PDS), as well as in the Core Leadership and Management Standards.

Examiners are expected to apply the '2 + 5 + 10 + M' framework (see page 35) to the evaluation of each script as a whole and to the evaluation of each answer. Assessing a script holistically against the '2 + 5 + 10 + M' yardsticks becomes crucial in the case of individuals at the borderline between pass and marginal fail, and at the borderline between fail and marginal fail. The critical questions asked when considering these borderline issues are:

- 'Are we prepared to see this individual going out into the world armed with the professional imprimatur of the CIPD?'

- 'Is this individual likely to perform in a manner which upholds both the vision of the CIPD and the strategic thinking performer aspirations of the Professional Development Scheme?'

If there is doubt about the response to this question, then a putative pass may be downgraded to marginal fail, and so on. What is vital for success, therefore, is an explicit demonstration of adherence to the *values* enshrined in the PDS, and possession of the *attitudes* that enable those values to be operationalised into *behaviour*. Indeed, the visible display of businesslike, strategically focused attitudes is more important than the occasional error of fact, or inability to reproduce detailed information about, say, some aspect of employment legislation. The PDS vision of the thinking performer is not principally about knowledge (although professional knowledge is, of course, important).

To cite a precise example, the May 2003 examination paper in People Resourcing (PR: the paper is reproduced on pages 133–138) included a question asking students to summarise and explain the new employment rights that came into effect in April 2003, and a second question that invited discussion about what the adjective 'good' might mean when applied to an organisation's employee. The vast majority of candidates, if selecting the employment rights question, were able to explore the topic at length and in depth, earning significant marks for themselves in the process. However, it was the second question – seeking views on what we might be visualising when we talk of someone as a 'good' employee – that really sought an expression of the thinking performer perspective, attitudes and values. For any candidate displaying marginal performance – a final mark hovering on the 48 or 49 levels – what would make the difference, in determining an overall pass is a high-quality, thinking-performer response to the 'good' employee question rather than a high-quality, comprehensive treatment for the question about the new employment rights. The employment rights question requires a demonstration of up-to-date knowledge, and although this is important (indeed, it is why a question was asked about it in the examination), it is less important than possession of appropriate attitudes that are consistent with the '2 + 5 + 10 + M' model.

Much the same situation was experienced with the May 2004 examination. Section B included a question about the legalities surrounding requests for flexible working, arising from the Employment Act 2002, but also questions about the cost-effective recruitment of graduates, about reasons for not moving a contact centre to India, and about accountability profiles. Many candidates answered the flexible working question very thoroughly indeed, but failed to write coherently about any of the other issues that involved consideration for the wider, strategic themes. Indeed, it was curious that some individuals who had advocated the introduction of accountability profiles (as an alternative and preferable to conventional job descriptions) in their treatment of the case study then demonstrated their complete ignorance about accountability profiles when addressing the relevant Section B question, by believing that accountability profiles are the same as competency frameworks, or by mistakenly believing that accountability profiles only apply to certain (usually higher-level) roles. As one person wrote: 'Accountability profiles are more suited to professional/managerial type roles ... It focuses on the aims of the role ... A job description is still relevant for some manual, repetitive roles.' No supporting evidence or rationale for this startling conclusion was advanced, yet when one thinks about it, why should not the aims of a role be just as applicable for manual, repetitive work as for any other form of employment? Arguably, accountability profiles are even more necessary for low-level work, where the overall purpose may be less self-evident.

So what does the "2 + 5 + 10 + M" formula actually involve?

- The 2 refers to the CIPD vision of the HR professional as a 'business partner' and a thinking performer. It is not necessary to rehearse here the arguments for a 'business partner' perspective, except to say that this has to be the way forward if the personnel/HR function is to be taken seriously, to exert significant influence in the organisation, to attract resources (physical, financial and human), and to offer exciting career opportunities to those entering it.

- The 5 are the five 'BACKUP' criteria linked specifically to the PDS Assessment system: business focus; application capability; knowledge of the subject matter; understanding in depth; and persuasion/presentation skills.

- The 10 are the 10 competencies listed in the PDS literature: personal drive and effectiveness; people management and leadership; business understanding; professional and ethical behaviour; added-value result achievement; continuing learning; analytical and intuitive/creative thinking; 'customer' focus; strategic thinking; and communication, persuasion and interpersonal skills.

- The 'M' are the performance expectations deriving from the fact that PR, like the entire CIPD Professional Standards framework, is a postgraduate qualification and therefore subject to the criteria conventionally applied to a Master's (hence 'M') programme.

This means that answers must characteristically go well beyond description and the reproduction of previously learned 'knowledge', and must instead demonstrate the capacity for critique, evaluation, analysis and dispassionate appraisal, deploying evidence-based argument in the process.

Specifically, what all this means is that each examination script is evaluated with a conspicuous preference for the following:

- *Evidence-based argument*: statements of 'fact' and personal belief should be reinforced by citations from appropriate third-party sources, research, and relevant literature (including one or more of the core textbooks).

- *Critical thinking*: this reflects the capacity to stand back from fashionable 'truths', conventional wisdom and the apparently authoritative pronouncements of even well-established 'experts' in order to assess genuine meanings and significance, to evaluate whether what is being said actually does make sense, and, most of all, to judge whether it would work in practice. Examiners also welcome the ability to make objective and impartial judgments about the real effectiveness (as opposed to the rhetoric) of resourcing policies, systems and practices in a given organisation, including the candidate's own.

- *Broad understanding of the PR field*: students must actively demonstrate a well-informed familiarity with the practice of PR not only within their own organisation and business sector, but also across a reasonable spectrum of organisations and sectors, especially those commonly acknowledged to be 'world-class' in the PR arena.

  Remember: it is not the purpose of the CIPD qualification simply to prepare students for efficient and effective performance in their current roles in their existing organisations, but rather to enable them to operate professionally within any HR role for any organisation in any sector. This is because (a) nobody can guarantee that their organisation will last forever, no matter how enduring it may seem, and (b) nobody can guarantee that their job will last forever, no matter how secure it might seem. In a world of turbulent uncertainty, the skills of 'employability' must apply not only to the labour market as a whole, but also to HR professionals.

• *Values that go beyond ethical/legal compliance*: compliance and process efficiency, though necessary for corporate survival, do not constitute a 'critical success factor' for high-performing people and organisations. Increasingly, both strategists and senior HR practitioners realise that high-performance working (originally developed as a concept for manufacturing industry, but now applied to all sectors) reflects a combination of infrastructure and differentiators. The infrastructure comprises the background systems that have to be in place merely to allow an organisation to function: adherence to the obligations of employment law, concern for diversity and equal opportunities, fair treatment for employees, efficient systems, and so forth. A competent infrastructure, however, will not deliver exceptional performance. It constitutes a range of what are known as 'critical failure factors', that is, elements of organisational life that can cause damage (generally financial, but also reputational) when they go wrong, but that do not promote excellence when they go right. To achieve excellence requires the kind of *differentiators* that are characterised in 'world-class' enterprises like Tesco, Nationwide, Selfridges, Pret a Manger, Lands' End Clothing, Cisco and so forth: the PR practices that reflect a restless search for something new, an interest in 'what works', a recognition that everyone in the business should 'add value', a belief in selecting for attitude rather than (merely) skill, and an overarching priority for mobilising every bit of talent that the workforce can supply.

In case there should be any misunderstanding, moreover, the entire '2 + 5 + 10 + M' framework is relevant to *all* those entering the PDS process, no matter how junior their position in any given organisation. Thus, entry into professional membership of the CIPD presupposes the capacity for strategic thinking, a 'business partner' perspective, and a breadth of critical understanding (to take some parts of the framework as examples): students must be able to demonstrate the connections between even a junior role and the organisation's strategic goals; they should be able to show how their activities 'add value'; and that their operational thinking extends further than the existing, conventional practices used within their own sector or enterprise.

To illustrate answers that do not exemplify the '2 + 5 + 10 + M' requirements, let us take one response to the May 2003 question about the meaning of 'good' when used in the context of people performance:

> They deliver what they are asked of in a timely manner. They are present at their desks for long hours. They do not bring lots of problems, so therefore they are easy maintenance. They are a likeable person.

There is no sense conveyed here of one who has absorbed a thinking performer perspective, or the notion of discretionary (organisational citizenship) behaviour, or the fashionable popularity of teamwork and group commitment. Indeed, the expectation that a 'good' employee will be present at his or her desk 'for long hours' is a manifestation of 'presenteeism' in action that is wholly antithetical to the pursuit of genuine employee excellence.

Another example may be cited from the November 2002 Employee Resourcing examination, which included a question about the 'select for attitude, train for skill' principle, inviting students to comment on its meaning and its potential application in their own environment. The opening paragraph from one answer reads as follows:

> My organisation is a local authority and have [sic] a very structured selection process based on qualifications, skills, experience and knowledge. This ensure [sic] that we meet our equal opportunity obligations and there is no discrimination against potential employees. 'Recruit for attitude, train for skill' would certainly be contrary to our practices as 'recruit for attitude' is quite subjective and can be open to discriminatory practices.

This material is unacceptable for a number of reasons. First, it demonstrates no awareness of the approaches used in other organisations – in some other local authorities, let alone large, reputable and even world-class employers in the private sector (such as Asda, Tesco, Lands' End Clothing, Nokia, First Direct, Microsoft, Pret a Manger and Egg), where attitude is the key capability sought and where no successful accusations of discrimination have ever been advanced. Second, it assumes that the systems used in the local authority that employs this student could not possibly be changed or improved.

Third, it is taken as axiomatic that the purpose of employee resourcing (ER) is to ensure that equal opportunity obligations are fulfilled and discrimination is avoided. But this is not so: the purpose of employee/people resourcing is to produce people who can willingly contribute to the furtherance of the organisation's goals and higher-order vision; legal/ethical compliance will not by itself enable this purpose to be achieved. Fourth, it is no argument against 'recruit for attitude, train for skill' to claim that it would be 'contrary' to the practices currently used in any given organisation. Students for the CIPD qualification are meant to be capable of assimilating and assessing new ideas for their potential value, irrespective of the degree to which these ideas are exhibited within existing procedures. This is what the thinking performer paradigm is crucially about.

I readily concede that there are many organisations that could not be characterised as contributor cultures, and where the notion of all employees as thinking performers would not be regarded as either credible or attractive. When an examination question on the subject was presented to ER students in 2001 (before the thinking performer vision had become central to the CIPD's qualification system), some of the answers were universally depressing and negative:

- 'This vision [of the thinking performer] would not be achievable in my organisation: the senior management are authoritarian and like it that way.'

- 'What the senior managers say [in my organisation] is not challenged. There is little or no employee participation or involvement. People are expected to do as they are told. Anyone who has their thoughts on how to do anything keeps these thoughts to themselves.'

- '[Getting our people to act as thinking performers] would cost a vast amount of money and waste valuable time.'

- 'In a production environment, [thinking performers] would be counter-productive because of the insistence on strict routines, tight procedural controls and close supervision.'

Equally, pan-European research by the Gallup Organisation, reported in *People Management* (Buckingham 2001) has suggested that genuinely engaged employees (in other words, thinking performers) constitute only around 17 per cent of the workforce, with a further non-engaged group making up 63 per cent and the rest (20 per cent) being 'disengaged', alienated, cynical, negative, unco-operative and hostile.

I acknowledge that some CIPD students find themselves working in such enterprises, and must therefore have difficulties in adopting the thinking performer values. However, the continued existence of workplaces where people are expected merely to conform to prescribed routines, where they are never consulted, where they are treated in effect as 'commodities', only serves to reinforce the desirability of the thinking performer framework and its associated values. If the UK economy were composed exclusively of organisations that not only tolerated but also actually celebrated maintenance of the status quo, then our national economic growth rate would be negligible, many companies would have gone out of business (faced with imaginative and entrepreneurial competition from overseas, if nowhere else), and many employees would survive in a permanent state of frustration and disappointment about their inability to 'make things happen'.

## What it takes to achieve success

To offer specific guidance when preparing for the PR examination I have chosen to highlight the five 'BACKUP' criteria and suggest some routes that will enable you to achieve (at a bare minimum) the necessary level of adequacy in your performance across all five:

- business focus

- application capability

- knowledge of the subject

- understanding in depth

- persuasion/presentation skills.

You must appreciate that success in this subject requires acceptable performance across all five competencies – you cannot trade off superb achievement in one against poor accomplishment in another, except in very minor ways that are unlikely to affect the final outcome.

As you embark on your study programme leading to the examinations, it is a good idea to assess yourself rigorously (along a 10-point scale, with zero indicating 'complete ignorance or inadequacy', and 10 implying complete command of the subject matter or the competency in question) against all five BACKUP criteria. If you are worried that your self-assessment may not be sufficiently objective, then of course it would be worthwhile to seek the opinions of others who know you well, and in particular your immediate manager or team leader.

The areas where you score low are those that require concentrated attention, and in undertaking your CPD activities throughout the study programme you should set yourself some learning goals for the BACKUP competencies where effort is most needed. If you have a personal tutor you should tell him or her what you are doing, and why: it may well be that he or she can help you, by providing some additional ways in which the selected competencies can be acquired or developed, and by supplying you with appropriate feedback from your assignments, practice case studies and other written work undertaken throughout the study programme.

Another key point is that you must set yourself the personal goal of attaining an examination mark of at least 60 per cent. Merely aiming for a pass (50 per cent) is too dangerous: as chief examiner I suspect that many candidates who were 'satisficing', that is, doing just enough work to 'get by' with a mark of 50 per cent, eventually fail the examination because on the day they do not perform at their best, or because they find that the mix of questions does not enable them to shine, or because they fail to address the case study in a productive manner. Conversely, if you aim to achieve 60 per cent you have equipped yourself with a safety margin and, what's more, you will feel more confident when you enter the examination room, so your performance will automatically improve anyway.

Now let us look through the five BACKUP competencies to see what is needed and how you can get there.

## Competency 1: business focus

This competency means that people are (actual or potential) value-added contributors to corporate purposes. The important question to ask about any employee is not 'What do you do?' but rather 'What are you for?' because strictly speaking nobody is employed to do anything – but they are employed to achieve results and deliver outputs. This is why job descriptions are so dangerous if they encourage employees to believe that what matters is the extent to which the tasks listed in the job description are performed, when what really matters is the attainment of key accountabilities and the central 'mission' of any given role. To take an example, checkout operators in a supermarket perform a range of tasks, but these are subordinate to their central 'mission', which may be 'to ensure that the customer wants to come back'.

A *business focus* also means that existing processes and procedures have to be evaluated against the expectation that they will add value, or at the very least that their benefits exceed their costs. Someone exhibiting business focus will frequently ask 'Why do we ...?' about current personnel/HR systems and conventional approaches, and 'Why don't we ...?' about the possibilities for reform, continuous improvement and change. Further, someone demonstrating business focus will be more interested in 'what works' than in mere compliance with the underpinning obligations of employment law.

A *business focus* implies some knowledge of 'big picture' issues, that is, the strategies associated with added-value PR. In recent examinations there have been case-study questions inviting candidates to develop PR strategies, and among a notable majority these requirements have been addressed very badly indeed. Some have ignored the matter altogether; many have simply written about operational changes like 'a graduate trainee programme', 'voluntary early retirement for employees nearing retirement age', 'absence management' and so forth (these examples are taken from selected treatments of the ANVIL case study in the May 2004 examination: see page 88). There is no space here to rehearse what is meant by a PR *strategy*, but it is a topic explored later in this revision guide. Suffice to say that the kind of transformational strategy expected for the ANVIL group (a company loosely modelled on BMW, by the way) could have involved some of these ingredients:

- creation of a collaborative, learning culture, to replace the 'blame culture' associated with the previous management

- substitution of 'facilitate-and-empower' for 'command-and-control'

- self-managed teams, with multi-skilling and job rotation as production demands change and also to break up the monotony of assembly-line work

- continuous improvement and change as built-in features of employee performance expectations (and therefore absorbed within the recruitment and selection processes)

- recruitment and selection activities founded on the search for positive 'attitudes'.

To develop your own capabilities in the business focus arena, here are some action-planning possibilities:

- Ask questions and collect information about the higher-order business purposes in your own organisation, and also within your department or function.

- Bearing in mind that by making a commitment to the PDS programme you have also made a commitment to career profes- sionalism across sectors other than the one in which you happen to be currently employed, collect all the literature and materials you can find about the links between PR and business focus in other organisations. If you work in the public sector, make a special point of learning about the private sector, and vice versa.

- Specifically seek out information from academic research that is relevant to this subject, such as the recent studies by Professor John Purcell of the University of Bath (Purcell *et al* 2003, and featured in a number of *People Management* articles – see the issue dated 15 May 2003). Purcell's investigations have concen- trated on the importance of what he calls the 'big idea' as a unifying force in the best-performing organisations.

- If you have Internet access, consult the search engines to learn what you can about organisations which have 'world-class' repu- tations both for results and for people effectiveness, such as Singa- pore Airlines, Tesco, First Direct, Nokia and Microsoft. (Please note, however, that these are only examples – there are plenty of others, that are not necessarily household names but that nonethe- less have managed to achieve impressive levels of integration between people commitment and organisational goals.)

- It is a good idea, too, to work collaboratively with others – perhaps colleagues in your study programme – to assemble and share information. If your study programme involves attendance at a college or university, it is likely that some of your fellow students will be employed by organisations where business focus among people (and among HR professionals) is well established, and you can learn from them – just as you can share your experience and knowledge with them. Here it is worth pointing out that passing the CIPD examinations is not a competitive exercise. Theoretically everyone could be successful, provided they met the CIPD professional standards. So, if you spread the study load by co-operating with others, you can all benefit and nobody is disadvantaged.

## Competency 2: application capability

*Application capability* refers to the talent for designing and presenting practical, cost-effective and business-relevant solutions to problems, plus decisive, innovative and imaginative actions for addressing opportunities. It is a competency that is tested principally through the case study – almost always you will be invited to produce recommendations as if to a senior executive or the chief executive officer – but it may also be relevant to some of the issues raised in Section B. For instance, the May 2003 PR paper included a question in which candidates were required to construct 'practical steps' that an organisation could take in order to address the 'problem' of retaining and promoting women.

Whatever recommendations you produce, they will be well received by the examiners if they are (a) directly and convincingly linked to the 'problem' you are trying to solve or the 'opportunity' you are trying to seize; (b) sufficiently detailed to enable the examiners to be persuaded that you know what you are writing about; and (c) accompanied by an authoritative rationale or cost–benefit calculation to show how implementing what you propose will lead to consequences that are advantageous not just to the organisation's employees but also to its overall performance (measured in terms of profitability, customer satisfaction or other credible factors).

By contrast, here are some examples of recommendations that were advanced by various candidates who entered the ER examination in November 2002 and whose case study responses included the following: 'Implement a good appraisal system', 'Introduce motivation themes', 'Ensure the correct training and development has taken place', and 'Implement management performance initiatives'.

As the chief examiner wrote at the time, how are we expected to know what a 'good appraisal system' looks like? What does it mean to 'introduce motivation themes'? Where do 'correct' training and development begin and end?

Another point is that even when students say the right thing (that is, produce statements that reflect the CIPD's values and the strategic vision of the thinking performer for the PDS), they will get no credit for doing so if their statements appear to be made up of nothing more than platitudinous rhetoric. Here is an example, again taken from the ER cohort in November 2002: 'The right people with the right skills required to add value and competitive advantage to the company. In today's turbulent, highly competitive market, flexible, innovative, high-performing employees are required. Thinking performers are the way forward.' This treatment manages to encapsulate virtually every high-sounding cliché in the current personnel/HR arena, but it says nothing convincing or credible in terms of application.

Yet a further consideration is that recommendations should be put forward assertively, confidently and authoritatively. If suggestions are advanced diffidently, then the reader begins to wonder if the author really believes in them. Thus one treatment of the ANVIL case study in the May 2004 examination wrote that the company should 'perhaps look at [sic] psychometric testing and assessment centres'. Nobody can be impressed by an apparent 'recommendation' which requires the HR director or CEO merely to 'look at' something, and then, to add insult to injury, tells them that they don't have to do so if they don't want to (which is the meaning to be attached to that little word, 'perhaps').

To develop your skills along the *application capability* continuum, you should be undertaking the following development initiatives:

- Especially if your current role does not require you ever to generate action proposals and recommendations, it is a good idea to consult with your manager, explain your need to acquire *application capability* credentials, and seek his or her co-operation in giving you a small-scale situation to investigate – perhaps the current car-parking arrangements, or the design of your job descriptions, or the layout of the personnel/HR department's reception area – so that you can practise your skills at generating credible routes for problem-solving and continuous improvement. In addition, producing a short project analysis about the situation you have investigated will help you with report-writing techniques. What you must do is take note of any feedback about the recommendations you produce and then implement the feedback with a second practice exercise.

- In preparing for the PR examination, it is essential that you undertake some rehearsal activities for the case study, by attempting some past case studies and then reviewing your work against the chief examiner's commentary included in his report on the examination results.

- Whenever you have produced some recommendations for dealing with a given situation (whether a case study or a 'real life' scenario), leave your work for 24 hours and then look at your proposals again. Ask yourself whether they are sufficiently precise, specific and informative to enable the imagined addressee to act on them as they stand; if they are not, then supply the necessary extra details. To say that an organisation needs 'a performance management system' is not helpful; to suggest that it should introduce a performance management system specifically targeted towards the customer services function, with targets focused on customer satisfaction, customer retention and customer referral, is much more authoritative.

- One very useful way to promote a sensible approach to the construction of meaningful recommendations, if you are part of a study programme with some fellow students, is to create a number of syndicate groups in order to address a typical case study, and then require each group to present its analysis and proposals to the rest of the cohort (who should act as the board or the central directorate of the organisation) – simultaneously making it clear that all suggestions for change or improvement must be challenged if ambiguous or seemingly unrelated to business purposes. Exposing yourself and your colleagues to peer review can be a powerful mechanism for performance development.

## Competency 3: knowledge of the subject matter

The chief examiner always recommends that students should be thoroughly familiar with about 50 per cent of the indicative content, and adequately familiar with the rest. The structure of the PDS examinations – a case study followed by a choice of seven from 10 shorter questions in Section B – makes the ancient art of 'question-spotting' much more difficult, if not impossible, and that, of course, is one of the principal reasons why the examination has that particular structure, because we want the examination to be a genuine test of student capability.

So candidates must become at least moderately acquainted with every topic from the indicative content. That means, too, that students must keep up to date, because it is entirely legitimate for the chief examiner to introduce question topics that may not have been mentioned directly in the indicative content but that have become 'hot' issues within the PR field. In recent examinations, questions have been asked about emotional intelligence, the so-called 'war for talent', and employer branding, even though none of these appeared in the 'syllabus'.

To acquire the expected degree of breadth of subject matter knowledge, you should be taking the following actions:

- At the commencement of your study programme, it is necessary to purchase a concertina file with about 20 separate compartments, and then give labels to each compartment derived from the principal areas of the indicative content, such as 'HR planning', 'Special case scenarios' and so forth. As your study unfolds, you should assiduously assemble materials from whatever sources are available to you – copies of *Personnel Management*, other HR or business periodicals (especially those available in your work location and/or reception area), items downloaded from the Internet, public-domain documents from your own organisation and from others (for example, recruitment literature, competency frameworks or performance appraisal system briefing notes), cuttings from the quality press and so on. Again, if you are attending a study programme in a college or university, you should set up a co-operative data-collection system with colleagues so that the productivity of your collective experience is maximised. Thus, if the class meets once weekly, everybody brings one item per week, with sufficient copies to enable the group to have one each. If tutors can be actively involved in this process, then so much the better.

- You must purchase a core textbook, either *People resourcing* by Stephen Taylor (CIPD) or *Employment resourcing* by Corbridge and Pilbeam (FT Publishing). Once you have obtained a book, it is then necessary to initiate a planned sequence of 'active reading' sessions to enable key parts of the text to be learned, because unfortunately the knowledge in the book will not transmit itself into your brain without your making a conscious effort to help the process along. In my view, 'active reading' sessions should not last for longer than an hour at a time, otherwise your concentration starts to wander, but you should schedule at least three such 'active reading' slots each week. For 'active reading' purposes, you must identify a quiet location, or wear earplugs if necessary, and remove all distractions, which might mean that you should sit at a table or a desk facing a featureless wall (do not sit where you can look out of the window, otherwise you may find things going on out there that will distract you from your purpose). Having chosen a key chapter, 'active reading' requires that you make notes, highlight quotations, underline key points, and in short do everything you can to guarantee that (a) you concentrate totally on the words in front of you, and (b) the information it contains enters your brain and remains there. After each 'active reading' hour, reward yourself with a small treat.

- In the period immediately prior to the examination, when you are revising, a key part of your revision activity must be a diligent review of the materials in your concertina file and the notes you made within each of your 'active reading' periods. It is advisable once more to use 'active reading' techniques at this point in your studies, too: that is, underlining, highlighting, taking notes, and even reading aloud if you find it helps in the memory-retention process.

## Competency 4: understanding in depth

The CIPD examinations are not so much a test of knowledge, but more a test of attitude and critical awareness. Rarely are any questions posed that call for nothing more than the reproduction of previously ingested information – almost always, students are invited first to describe, but then to explain, to evaluate, to analyse, to assess. This is why it is so healthy for candidates to adopt a permanently questioning mentality (even if such a mentality is not always welcomed when displayed in the work environment), and of course, such a mentality is appropriate in a professional context because of the general expectation that personnel/ HR practitioners must continue to innovate and to challenge.

Possession of a critical understanding, too, is a requirement of the PDS given that it is a postgraduate qualification that is subject to what are known as the 'M-level' descriptors, namely, that students must display:

* a systematic understanding of knowledge and a critical aware-ness of current problems and/or new insights

* a comprehensive understanding of techniques

* originality in the application of knowledge

* a conceptual understanding that enables both current research and methodologies to be evaluated critically

* the ability to deal with complex issues both systematically and creatively, make sound judgments in the absence of complete data, and communicate conclusions

* the demonstration of self-direction and originality in tackling and solving problems, plus the willingness to act autonomously in planning and implementing tasks

* a continued drive to advance knowledge, understanding and skills (principally through CPD).

So here are some ways in which understanding can be acquired and developed within a study programme leading to the CIPD examinations:

* Undertaking the 'active reading' sessions, as outlined above, should enable you to assimilate some of the required mentality

since it is demonstrated at length in both of the textbooks identified by name.

- Critical faculties are enhanced when individuals learn to seek authoritative evidence for statements and apparently factual propositions that may reflect nothing more than conventional wisdom. For instance, it is commonly believed that one-to-one selection interviews present opportunities for psychological prejudice, the 'halo effect' and subjective judgements, yet these phenomena are absent, or relatively absent, from the panel interview. Equally, it may be argued that if two or three people are involved in candidate selection, either as panel members or in a sequence of one-to-one interviews, then multiplicity of numbers moves the final decision nearer to absolute objectivity. There is not a shred of evidence to support either of these conclusions. Lots of evidence, on the other hand, exists to show that the traditional selection interview has a very low predictive validity, yet many interviewers regard themselves as exceptions to this general rule, and will reject the evidence or even pretend that it does not exist. The budding personnel/HR professional must cope with these (sometimes emotive) issues, but must continue to challenge, to search for worthwhile evidence, and to promote a dispassionate approach to the creation of action-planning options.

- In addressing examination questions where it is appropriate for third-party sources of evidence and research to be cited, it is now, more than ever, important for CIPD students to incorporate such references into their answer treatments. It is not enough simply to write, 'Research has indicated that ...'; instead, candidates must be able to point out that 'Research by Marcus Buckingham, reported in *People Management* (October 2001), concludes that only about 17 per cent of employees are genuinely "engaged" in their work and within their organisations.'

As examples of the general point being advanced here, one need look no further than some treatments of the ANVIL case study in the May 2004 examination. The second part of the exercise called for recruitment and selection systems that would aid the company in its search for transformational performance. Many 'solutions' were disappointingly conventional, predicated by nothing more than a traditional, systematic approach to recruitment and selection involving job analysis, job descriptions, person specifications, and elaborate interviews, but what is more to the point in the present context is that one person wrote, 'The interview would be with two people; when one person carries out the interview it can be very subjective and partial [sic] to the halo/horns effect'. Not a shred of supporting evidence was produced to justify this claim, or the implicit belief that somehow an interview conducted by two people would be less subjective.

## Competency 5: presentation and persuasion skills

It is true that relatively little attention is paid by the examiners to the presentation of answers within Section B, especially as students have relatively little time in which to consider the technicalities of layout and design if they have to produce seven answers within an hour. Even so, it has to be admitted that material that is 'reader-friendly' does convey a better impression than pages that are difficult to decipher, disorganised and incoherent. With Section A, the case study, this is even more important, because characteristically candidates are required to produce their responses in the form of a report addressed to, say, the chief executive or the HR director, so some adherence to the canons of businesslike report writing is expected. On the other hand, there is no guarantee that every case study scenario will require the answer to be produced as a report: in the recent past, candidates have been asked for 'action guidelines' to be presented to franchise holders for a chain of beauty and body therapy shops, and detailed 'briefing notes' for the recruitment and selection of customer service assistants at petrol stations. Unfortunately some individuals, evidently well-trained in report writing, persist in producing reports even when specifically required not to do so, and lose marks accordingly for their refusal to adhere to instructions.

If a report is requested, candidates should adhere broadly speaking to the following presentational criteria:

- Begin with a title page, having selected a title that summarises what the report is supposed to be about, that is, its purposes (rather than its content).

- An outline contents page should follow, although in the context of an examination the page numbers are likely to be fictional rather than authentic. At least the contents summary should give an indication of the report structure, with section or chapter titles, especially embracing 'Conclusions' and 'Recommendations' (these must be treated separately and not amalgamated).

- It is desirable, though not compulsory, to produce a short, one-paragraph 'Summary' of the report as a whole, not just its recommendations.

- Usually, the section/chapter titles will begin with an 'Introduction' and possibly a 'Method of investigation' paragraph, followed by 'Findings'. However, the word 'findings' should not be used: it is far preferable to select titles that are more closely linked to the subject matter.

- Within each section, material should be organised in short paragraphs and/or sub-paragraphs, numbered sequentially, with some cross-referencing where appropriate. It is definitely not appropriate to develop the text as if writing an essay, since it then becomes more difficult for the busy reader to disentangle analysis from description, and inference from recommendation.

- Recommendations should be as detailed and specific as possible, preferably prioritised, and accompanied by a short cost–benefit evaluation. If the case study brief has called for separate questions to be answered, then the material in the report should be similarly separated.

- There are certain verbal and phrase formulations that are to be avoided, especially in the 'Recommendations'. If the word 'hopefully' is used, it implies that the author is uncertain about either the recommendation itself or its consequences – and this is not the way to convince the imagined reader that the proposal is likely to work. Equally undesirable is 'I feel', 'I would suggest' and similar variants, as the executive to whom the report is addressed should not be interested in the author's 'feelings' but rather in the degree of dispassionate situational analysis that has been undertaken.

- It is far preferable, therefore, for students to adopt a confident, assertive style for both the 'recommendations' and also the content of answers generally. Proposals for action can be much more authoritative if they are reinforced by meaningful research references or by the citation of other corporate instances where similar ideas have already been implemented with conspicuous success.

Pre-examination practice with report writing and indeed with examination techniques as a whole is an essential part of the study programme. Initially, I recommend that you address one or two past PR/ER case studies but do so without feeling the need to adhere to strict time limits, since the important skill to develop is proficiency in situational analysis, problem-solving and continuous improvement.

With the ANVIL case study that featured in the May 2004 examination, for example, a report structure that could have worked very well might have been organised along the following lines:

1. *A brief introduction* (no more than a single page) – summarising the key issues currently confronted by the ANVIL group, the progress already made, and the vision yet to be attained.

2. *The resourcing strategies that ANVIL should pursue* (in response to the first question in the 'terms of reference') – these should have been based on the experiences of high-performance organisations, so this part of the report would have had two sub-sections, 'High-performance working', and 'Recommendations'.

3. *The barriers* – in gaining acceptance for these strategies.

4. *Overcoming the barriers* – through consultation, involvement, some accelerated senior-level departures if some executives lack commitment to the new values, and so forth.

5. *Implementing the strategy through recruitment and selection* – again with two sections, one to present the alternatives plus the factors to be considered, and one to consist of some clear, incisive recommendations.

Note that this proposed design (which is presented here merely as one acceptable model, not as the sole legitimate approach) is derived from the task portrayed in the case study brief and is not dependent on any preconceived report writing model. Thus there is no use of such headings as 'Main body', 'Findings' or other generic categories. Unfortunately, the reality demonstrates that some individuals, coached into writing reports with such broad-based headings, persist in doing so even when with a little effort they could customise their material; others appear not to be at all familiar with the practice of businesslike communications. Sometimes it is hard to detect any adherence to the 'terms of reference', sometimes the recommendations are hidden within the 'report' itself, sometimes the headings used, if any, are seemingly unconnected to the subject matter. There is no excuse for such elementary incompetence.

## How to succeed

Apart from adherence to the underpinning thinking performer and the CIPD's 'business partner' vision, it is essential that you show the examiners that you have attained an appropriate level of proficiency across all five of the BACKUP criteria which now form an indispensable part of the evaluation process. To do this, your work must actively demonstrate your allegiance to the BACKUP factors – which means that as the examiners assess your answers, they must be persuaded to supply positive responses to as many of the following performance-related questions as possible.

### Business orientation

- Does the individual appear to recognise that people are principally employed as actual or potential contributors to wider corporate purposes, and not merely as self-contained ends in themselves?

- Is there some acknowledgement of the central importance of higher-order strategic goals in organisations as the foundation from which PR processes should be constructed?

- Has the requirement for people to 'add value' been internalised?

- Does the individual know how to create and implement PR

procedures in order to make it more likely that an 'added value' climate or 'contributor culture' will be created?

- Does the individual understand that the real customers for PR professionals are the central directorate of whatever organisation employs them?

## Application capability

- Where recommendations and action proposals are asked for, are they supplied?

- Are the recommendations sufficiently explicit to enable the reader to know exactly what is being advocated, and why? Do they, in other words, pass the 'so what' test?

- Do the recommendations appear to be sensibly and logically linked to any preceding analysis? Are they cogent, cost-justified and credible from the point of view of the visualised addressee?

- Are the recommendations persuasive when tested against the situation described in the case study brief?

- Are the recommendations presented assertively, with confidence and authority?

## Knowledge of the subject matter

- Does the individual have sufficient breadth of awareness of the coverage within the indicative content, including new major topics and themes not specifically mentioned therein?

- Is it apparent that knowledge of the field extends outside the individual's immediate work organisation and business sector?

- Can we see some familiarity with PR innovations, initiatives and new or experimental approaches being practised or developed by leading-edge and 'world-class' organisations and employers?

## Understanding in depth

- Is there evidence of the exercise of the individual's own critical faculties, enabling so-called 'facts' in the PR arena and current conventional wisdom to be challenged, albeit constructively?

- Do the ideas and suggestions produced by the individual show that he or she is prepared to go beyond process, legal and ethical compliance factors in order to focus crucially on ways in which PR can be undertaken more efficiently (for example, with quicker response and decision-making times) and also more effectively (for example, with higher quality outputs, more successful selection decisions, improved levels of employee retention, and so forth)?

- Can the individual think 'outside the box', when encouraged to do so, in order to develop some original approaches to PR issues?

**Presentation and persuasion skills**

- Is answer material properly thought out, thought through and systematically developed, so that arguments can be followed sequentially to their natural conclusions and action implications?

- Is any use made of evidence from cited third parties as sources of supporting data and experiential corroboration, organisational vignettes, and so forth, in order to add credibility to the points being made?

- With the case study in particular, is the treatment presented as specified in the brief, that is, as a report to the chief executive if required, or as managerial guidance notes if required, and so forth?

- Does the answer – again for the case study in particular – take account of the likely values of the visualised addressee, including any 'political' factors, which may mean that the language and ideas have to be carefully chosen?

# How to fail

It may seem depressing to reflect on the possibility of failure – yet it does remain true that around one-third of those taking the national examinations in PR do not succeed. This is not because there is some pre-ordained pass rate: the chief examiner has often repeated the point that if all examination candidates met the CIPD's standards, then everyone could pass. There is nothing he or she would like better.

But the unfortunate reality is that it is very rare in any examination system for every candidate to pass – and when it does occur, some observers, whether justified or not, immediately suspect the validity and reliability of the system. Over the years, I have come to the conclusion that it is also very rare for individuals to fail the examination because they cannot cope with examinations – in other words, to fail for reasons that in a sense are beyond their control. Let us therefore face the truth:

• If you succeed in this (or any other) examination, the responsibility for that success is yours and yours alone – even if you did have some tutorial help along the way.

It therefore follows that:

• If you fail in this (or any other) examination, the responsibility for that failure is yours and yours alone – and it is better to accept that reality, and act accordingly, than to attempt to blame others.

Here is a list of the most common causes of failure. Only one of them will produce a 'fail' outcome on its own; in the case of the others, it is a combination of the causes that makes the difference. You need to know about these causes (just as you may need to know the most probable causes of certain diseases), because you can then take action (lifestyle or diet changes if it is a feared disease we are talking about) to make sure that these causes do not apply to you.

## The one cause that inevitably means you will fail

You are guaranteed to fail if you do not attempt all seven required questions in Section B, irrespective of the marks you may secure for your other Section B responses, the mark you are awarded for your Section A case study treatment, and the mark you accumulate for the examination as a whole. This is because the examination is designed to test you against the '2 + 5 + 10 + M' formula, and some of these ingredients cannot accurately be evaluated if you do not fulfil the precise requirements of the examination structure. Clearly the obligation to undertake a case study for one hour, plus seven shorter questions in the second hour, is achievable, because the vast majority of candidates achieve it, so it is incumbent upon all students to manage their time efficiently to enable the CIPD's specification to be met.

## The other causes that make a difference

First, people fail because they do not demonstrate adherence to the core 'business partner' and 'thinking performer' values. Instead, they write as if PR were a self-contained activity governed largely, if not exclusively, by the need to adhere to the requirements of employment law, but not answerable to any strategic purposes or 'added value' expectations.

Second, people fail because they are conspicuously deficient in their knowledge of the subject matter. Maybe they thought merely to 'satisfice' (that is, do just enough to 'get by' in passing the examination) and misjudged the amount of subject matter knowledge they would need; maybe they were motivated instrumentally by the desire to obtain the CIPD qualification rather than by the desire for professional competency; a few could simply have misinterpreted the whole philosophy and level at which the PDS Standards operate.

Third, people fail because their scripts betray no sign whatsoever of any recourse to convincing third-party evidence. In his 2004 book, *The knowing–doing gap*, Jeffrey Pfeffer wrote:

> If taken seriously, evidence-based management can change how every manager thinks and acts. It is a way of seeing the world and using business knowledge that can drive every firm to make better decisions, take wiser decisions and, as a side benefit, treat people better.

An expectation that answers will be reinforced by evidence has been part of the PDS since its inception, but we are still some way away from total acceptance of its implications. From the May 2004 cohort, as on previous occasions, there were still significant numbers of scripts which contained *no references whatsoever* to any third-party sources, research, named organisations, articles from periodicals, or even core textbooks. (Incidentally, it is not sufficient for answers to be peppered with vague phrases like 'Research shows/proves/

suggests ...' or 'Recent research has indicated ...'. Although citations do not have to be articulated in comprehensive detail, the examiners do expect that the name(s) of the researcher(s) will be given, and the year of publication for their findings, for example, 'The Purcell "black box" studies of 2003 ...'.)

Fourth, people fail because their material does not acknowledge any strategic or 'big-picture' perspective about PR. The May 2004 case study, itself modelled on BMW's experiences at the previous British Leyland factory in Oxford, sought guidance on the design of a transformational resourcing strategy, yet it became apparent that (a) many did not know what a 'PR strategy' might contain or look like, and (b) many could not separate 'strategy' from 'practice' in any meaningful way. I appreciate that many CIPD students may be employed in roles that are largely if, not exclusively, operational in character, but this does not excuse their apparent indifference to the strategic imperatives that underpin (or that should underpin) their activities. True, candidates often tell me that they find strategy 'boring', but perhaps this is because they think that strategy does not touch their everyday lives. In reality it should, and individuals should be able to trace a connection between their organisation's strategic direction, their organisation's HR strategies, and their own contribution to these strategic goals. Perhaps the clearest example concerns customer service, because if a company elects to differentiate itself in the marketplace through 'world-class' customer service (a strategic imperative), then this has clear implications for the company's recruitment, selection, induction, learning/development, reward/recognition/review processes, all of which may have to be modified to take account of this new focus.

Fifth, people fail because they seem not to be aware of innovative PR in organisations and sectors other than their own. Yet learning about high-performance organisations – as exemplars of what can be done in the resourcing arena – is not difficult. Information is readily available about such companies as Tesco and Nationwide in the Purcell 'black box' research (Purcell *et al* 2003); recent *People Management* articles about, say, BMW and Pret a Manger can be downloaded from the CIPD website; generalised Internet searches can reveal useful material; and it is even possible to elicit worthwhile data from the websites run by these organisations themselves, especially if they deploy online recruitment processes.

## Some final thoughts

In 1993, the Personnel Standards Lead Body commissioned some
research in an effort to discover what chief executives thought about
the personnel/HR function and its typical practitioners. The
research identified some negative perceptions, which, I am afraid,
still exist (with justification) in certain quarters and in certain
organisations:

- Some personnel/HR professionals seem to think more about the
  exercise of their professional skills than about the extent to
  which they could make a positive strategic and operational
  contribution to the organisation by which they are employed.

- Many demonstrate an over-conscious concern for rules, procedures and employment law, to the point where they appear to
  take a positive delight in raising objections to proposed managerial initiatives rather than in facilitating the translation of such
  initiatives into tangible outcomes.

- HR/personnel professionals are often enthusiastic about introducing systems and procedures that fail because they are not
  sufficiently tailored to meet the needs of the business and also
  because they are not owned by management.

- In many enterprises, the function adopts an indiscriminate
  approach to being a 'good employer', unrelated to, say, the precise
  circumstances of the labour market in a given environment and
  the resources available to the organisation.

Even if some of these criticisms are founded on mistaken stereo-
types as opposed to hard evidence, it is imperative to undermine
such impressions where they continue – and consistent adoption
of the thinking performer perspective and a contributor culture
will both contribute to the attainment of a new vision. Here are
some key mistakes often made by students when they implicitly
portray an isolationist, insular, 'professional' perspective uninformed by any genuine concern for the real world and the
corporate context:

- Proposing recommendations for action that say nothing about
  costs and nothing about the business benefits.

- Where benefits are outlined, assessing them solely against 'professional' criteria.

- Adoption of an assumed paradigm of 'best practice' without regard for organisational realities. Although the term 'good practice' is acceptable, 'best practice' suggests an idealistic, utopian state of affairs to which all enterprises should aspire, and a scenario that therefore militates against innovation. Indeed, 'best practice' often refers to nothing more than adherence to a systematic recruitment/selection model – HR planning, job analysis, job descriptions, person specifications, and so forth – which is not the framework conventionally adopted by 'world-class' companies.

- The implication that the personnel/HR function is a self-contained entity rather than a positive contributor to the fulfilment of a strategic vision and the organisation's competitive advantage in its wider marketplace.

Getting it right, by contrast, involves these key considerations – which apply not just within the PDS examinations but also in the practical realities of career success:

- Answers in the examination must emphasise a close degree of integration between people management, the HR/personnel function, and the imperatives of the 'business' (whether in the private sector or elsewhere, since increasingly public-sector organisations are measured against private-sector priorities).

- Equally, answers must demonstrate a genuine concern about meeting the requirements of the 'customers' who ultimately pay for the presence of PR professionals and whose opinions therefore count (or should count) for a great deal. (When the chief examiner asked a short question recently in which students were invited to indicate the 'customers' for PR, many wrote about job applicants and other 'stakeholders', but few considered it relevant to suggest that perhaps the proper role for PR professionals is to create and administer recruitment and selection systems that make it easier for the organisation's board of directors to achieve their stated strategic and aspirational goals for the enterprise. Thus, if the business has decided to make customer service its competitive advantage, and wants this focus to form part of every employee's toolkit, then customer service must be written into job descriptions and accountability profiles, become part of person specifications and competency frameworks, and form a key dimension of the recruitment and selection system in the way it treats applicants.)

- When formulating recommendations, especially within the case study, candidates should acknowledge the likelihood that at least some of their proposals will have to encounter implementation barriers. These should be mentioned, and a brief account given of the ways in which such barriers could be overcome or minimised in practice.

- Linked to this same argument is the fact that CIPD students (no matter how young and innocent) need to demonstrate their awareness of the 'political' realities of organisational life. In many instances from the recent past, where a Section A case study has specified that the answer is to be written in the form of a report for the chief executive officer, individuals have included in their recommendations the statement that the chief executive officer should be dismissed or coerced into early retirement. Such suggestions are frequently unwise; if the departure of the chief executive officer is desirable (as it sometimes is), then this is a course of action that has to be presented with tact and sensitivity, often with a dignified escape route provided.

- Examination answers should contain fewer references to 'professionalism' and 'best practice', but more about 'business benefits', 'continuous improvement', 'competitive advantage' and 'cross-sector benchmarking'.

- One further key factor which candidates would do very well to bear in mind is that the chief examiner can only judge what appears in the answer book, because he has no other information available to him or her about the student's state of mind, the amount of information residing in the student's brain (though not reproduced in the answer book), and what the student might have said had more time been available. This means that *candidates must sell themselves as vigorously as possible*: knowledge, understanding and other capabilities can only be assessed by the extent to which they have been demonstrated explicitly. Relatively few individuals make it clear that they have read any source materials, not even the CIPD textbook; relatively few mention their own work experiences; few cite any third-party sources of evidence or research, or any benchmark applications of 'good practice' in the field of PR. Students who behave in this fashion are making it more difficult for themselves, because in the 'shop window' of the answer book they have deliberately chosen to turn the lighting off and keep their 'goods' under wraps.

There are some specific issues with regard to examination technique, moreover. With every diet, there are significant numbers of candidates who begin by addressing Section B (seven questions within an hour), write at excessive length on some topics, and then leave themselves with insufficient time to do justice to the case study. It is more sensible to devote the pre-examination reading time to a thorough scrutiny of the case study brief and then, when writing commences, make some notes before embarking on the answer itself, especially as the majority of Section B questions, though requiring thought, are typically more straightforward and can be tackled without so much cerebral preparation. It is also important to remember that the two halves of the examination are meant to complement each other, especially as they confront differing competencies, and the examiner does not allow an excellent result for Section B to compensate for inadequate achievement in Section A, or vice versa.

Conscientious and efficient management of the available time has to be an important skill for the CIPD examinations. For this reason alone, some pre-examination practice will pay dividends, but there are other considerations as well. These days, very few people use handwriting at work or anywhere else – they are much more likely to operate a keyboard – yet until we can guarantee the universal availability of word processors in examination centres, we have to require CIPD candidates to produce their answers in longhand. This process can be physically exhausting, particularly for individuals unaccustomed to such activity, and practice to build up the necessary muscles would be time well spent.

Bearing in mind the performance criteria expected from a thinking performer, then a 'good' Section B answer will generally include elements of knowledge display, critical evaluation, third-party referencing (from relevant research or literature, such as the textbook), and an attempt to link the question theme to the student's own work experience or to a named organisational scenario. Of course, not all Section B topics lend themselves to this somewhat simplistic model, but most do and this should be the prescription adopted.

Last but very definitely not least, it is essential to answer the question. When estate agents are asked about the top three factors that determine the price and value of a piece of property, they usually reply, 'location, location, location'. Similarly, answering the question needs to be emphasised three times: answer the question, answer the question, answer the question. Marks will not be given for content, however well informed, if it is unrelated to the central issues, and marks will not be given for superfluous material, like words of greeting or farewell. Section B of the PDS examination for PR is structured round 10 e-mail messages, and candidates must select seven, showing how they would respond. Despite the fact that the rubric for the examination paper clearly states what is expected ('You are required to indicate the content of your proposed response'), some have found it necessary to produce entirely gratuitous remarks, such as 'Sorry for the delay in replying, I have just got back from a meeting' or 'Hi, sorry, I meant to come and talk to you about this.'

## Conclusion

In preparing for the examination there are many points to consider and many guidelines to follow, but perhaps unfortunately there are no quick and easy routes to success (if there were, they would have been discovered by now). However, if you act on the advice contained in these notes, you will deserve to succeed and you will undoubtedly do so, and the lessons learned will be invaluable to you throughout your subsequent career.

# 3 EXAMINER'S INSIGHTS

## Introduction

Within the framework already described earlier in this revision guide, the chief examiner specified the following detailed ingredients as the basis for assessing student performance:

**Positive**

- Demonstrates *business focus* through a good understanding of HR/corporate strategy.

- Appears sensitive to wider 'political' and organisational issues.

- Equipped with *application capability*, generating recommendations that are cogent, specific and convincing.

- At least some recommendations show evidence of original and innovative thinking

- Confronts implementation problems – in other words, shows how 'big-picture' recommendations could be translated into operational and tangible actions.

- Shows thorough *knowledge of the relevant subject matter.*

- Reinforces knowledge with *critical understanding* – challenges conventional wisdom and current practices.

- Adequate inclusion of references to third-party sources, such as relevant literature, research evidence and so forth.

- Draws on appropriate organisational examples to show good practice or world-class benchmarking possibilities and potential.

- Makes use of own work experience scenarios in analytical fashion, going beyond mere description.

- Answers are well presented and persuasive, lucid and articulate, especially the case study.

**Negative**

- Absence of *business orientation* – appears to be driven by 'professional' priorities and abstract, indiscriminate personnel/HR imperatives.

- No coherent *application capability* – relies on general, undeveloped platitudes unrelated to the task in hand.

- *Knowledge of the subject matter* poor, demonstrating a mixture of ignorance and significant factual mistakes.

- No evidence of *critical understanding*, with answers largely confined to superficial description and low-level analysis.

- Few or no references to relevant third-party evidence and/or organisational examples (not even the core textbook).

- *Persuasion and presentation* poor, with arguments difficult to follow, material hard to read, unelaborated bullet points, lack of co-ordination between 'Findings', 'Conclusions' and 'Recommendations'.

- Answers typically too discursive, betraying lack of focus on the key issues to be addressed.

The results from the May 2003 entry indicate that there is some way to go before the performance expectations associated with the Professional Development Scheme (PDS) will be fully absorbed, particularly so far as critical understanding and the thinking performer paradigm are concerned. In what follows I have summarised the key issues, initially for the examination as a whole, then for each section, and ultimately for the specific questions themselves.

## The key issues: the examination as a whole

The chief examiner and colleagues in his marking team rigorously applied the '2 + 10 + 5' assessment criteria to each script (see Preface). It was also seen as important to view each candidate's script with the postgraduate or 'M'-level requirements in mind. Thus any statements of 'fact' should have been reinforced by citations from appropriate third-party sources, and there should be evidence of the willingness to challenge conventional wisdom or even research findings. (Not all research findings are factual merely because they have resulted from research – in many cases the methodologies may be flawed, the samples unrepresentative, and the analysis characterised by wishful thinking.) Candidates were also expected to exhibit a well-informed understanding of the practice of personnel/HR outside their immediate organisational and business sector, and should not have been narrowly focused on ethical/legal compliance as the ultimate measure of HR performance.

Against these criteria, the following considerations deserve your attention (given that you are presumably reading this as a future examination candidate for PR):

1. A significant proportion of scripts continue to contain no references whatsoever to any sources of evidence, research, a textbook or third-party material of any kind. From the evidence, therefore, the chief examiner would be entitled to conclude that such students had undertaken no reading, little preparation, and had certainly not taken advantage of, say, Stephen Taylor's excellent book *People resourcing*. Since the inclusion of citations from external sources is now a critical feature of PDS expectations, then students who do not incorporate such material in their scripts must stand little chance of success.

2. It is not enough simply to produce vague phrases like 'Research indicates ...' or 'Research suggests ...' or even 'Research from various sources suggests ...'. Although citations from such populist periodicals as *Personnel Today* are better than nothing, they are still not taking the issue of evidence-based argument far enough.

3. Occasionally candidates continue to harm their chances of success by excelling in one part of the examination while performing disastrously in the other. The CIPD rules clearly state that anyone will fail if they are awarded fewer than 40 per cent of the available marks in either section. (This rule was deliberately created in order to ensure that a comprehensive range of competencies is tested.)

# The key issues: Section A

The case study treatment was marked out of 100, with up to 50 marks for each of the two specific questions posed. There was no specific mark allocation for presentation quality, that is, the organisation of the answer material into a structured report (as specified in the brief), but this element was taken into account when awarding marks more generally. It was expected that in the first question – about the difficulties of culture change – students would concentrate on the people resourcing (PR) aspects, that is, new specifications about the role for people, new types of recruitment and selection techniques, new approaches to motivation, leadership and performance management, and so forth. (The question is reproduced on page 84.) If examples of relevant culture change were to be used to reinforce this part of the answer treatment, they could have been found in organisations that have decided to outsource their back-office functions to a specialist provider, possibly operating overseas, or in those which have replaced full-time, long-serving staff by fixed-term contractual employees, or in companies that have moved from centralised paternalism to devolved empowerment (for example, Sainsbury's).

So far as the second question was concerned, there were 50 marks available for the answer as a whole, which needed to address all three specified themes: the proposed competency framework for the 'consultant' role, the selection methods to be used, and the action to be taken in the case of existing supervisors who either did not want to be, or lacked the capabilities of becoming, 'consultants' themselves. Anyone failing to cover any one of the three themes automatically sacrificed approximately 15 marks; further marks could have been lost if individuals ignored the requirement that recommendations should be reinforced by references to appropriate research material and benchmarking evidence from other organisations.

In practice, some of the key learning points for future students will have to be derived from these observations:

1.  Despite the fact that the 'terms of reference' was clearly divided into two separate topic areas, some answers did not conform to this obligation – and so dividing the 'report' into its component parts merely added gratuitously to the chief examiner's task.

2.  As the Professional Qualification Scheme has evolved incremen-
    tally (but also transformationally) into the PDS, one constant
    feature has remained, namely, the virtual inevitability of the fact
    that case study answers should be structured as a report. A
    significant proportion of candidates continue to ignore this
    requirement: they produce no title page, no contents page, no
    introduction, no clearly delineated recommendations, or no
    distinction between 'findings' and 'conclusions'.

3.  In terms of writing style, too, many do not organise their text
    into numbered paragraphs and sub-paragraphs, but prefer to
    present their thoughts as an undifferentiated stream of
    consciousness, facts mixed up with interpretation, conclusions
    mixed up with recommendations, and topics addressed haphaz-
    ardly throughout. (This difficulty can easily be resolved if a
    'rough plan' is produced before the answer proper is written.)
    Paragraphs can easily become over-long (a page or so), and the
    resultant material is very definitely not reader-friendly.

4.  The chief examiner in the past has criticised the apparent
    reluctance of many candidates to generate assertive, decisive
    and confident proposals for action, but unfortunately this
    continues to be a difficulty. Two examples (from separate
    scripts) will suffice: 'Look at the possibility of consultants with
    expertise in change management to help introduce as smoothly
    as possible,' and 'It may be a good idea to run an assessment
    centre.' As you are reading this, imagine what your reactions
    would be if you had commissioned this report and the author
    had presented you with recommendations as weak, hesitant and
    indecisive as these – and then ask yourself how the recommen-
    dations could be changed to make them more acceptable. It's not
    difficult, is it?

5.  The two tasks were to be undertaken as a service to the chief exec-
    utive of your company, Dr Tomkinson, who wishes to introduce
    an IMS-type culture into his own business. Task 1 asked for a
    review of the problems associated with a shift of PR philosophies,
    plus 'some evidence-based proposals about how to make the
    changes easier to accomplish and assimilate'. Task 2 sought
    advice about 'the methods of implementing the new philosophy'.

It was surprising and disappointing, therefore, that so many individuals devoted much of their available time and space to what
can only be described as an exercise in negativity. For them, the
problems were enormous and virtually insuperable, and the
provision of constructive help, plus a 'can do' attitude, was
noticeably absent. Future students would do well to remember
that if they are to add value in their organisations, it is their
principal role to assist in the furtherance of stated corporate goals,
and although it is legitimate to articulate concerns about the
difficulties, it is not appropriate to dwell on them indefinitely.

6.  More specifically, the obligation to produce a competency
    framework for the new 'consultant' role was a cause of many
    difficulties – even though several case studies in the PQS
    Employee Resourcing examination have also focused on compe-
    tencies, many organisations currently use competency frame-
    works (instead of person specifications), and there has been
    extensive literature about competencies, published by the CIPD
    and in *People Management*. If a competency-based approach is to
    work, then each competency has to be defined in some detail,
    and so vague (unelaborated) titles like 'Understanding', 'Knowl-
    edge' and 'Diversity' are totally inadequate. Several scripts
    simply offered a list of so-called competencies without any
    supporting explanation or rationale at all; and a significant
    minority avoided the issue altogether, claiming instead that 'A
    competency framework must be put together', but omitting to
    indicate what it could comprise.

7.  The 'terms of reference' sought evidence-based proposals
    (because this is now part of the performance expectation associ-
    ated with the PDS, although of course proposals derived from
    evidence should be a normal aspect of any advocacy advanced
    by a properly performing personnel/HR practitioner anyway).
    This is a requirement that a large number of examination candi-
    dates have yet to take seriously. Instead, many recommenda-
    tions were advanced as if the case for their implementation was
    self-evident, for example, the use of assessment centres, psycho-
    metric testing, work practice tests, 'tandem interviews with two
    to three people present to give a more objective view', emotional
    intelligence capability evaluation, and so on. Frankly, such a

cavalier approach will not in future be acceptable. If the use of assessment centres is being promoted or defended, then students must seek to show how the costs involved (particularly as they are considerable) can be justified against the potential benefits of improved predictive validity in the selection process; glib references to 'psychometric testing' must be reinforced with an indication of their scope and scale; work practice tests must be accompanied by a brief acknowledgement of the research evidence about their usefulness; the assumption that interviews involving two or three people are somehow 'more objective' should be vigorously challenged; and the fashionable enthusiasm for emotional intelligence has to be tempered by some notes of analytical caution.

# The key issues: Section B

For PR, the Section B questions are presented as a collection of e-mail messages for which suitable responses must be devised. (A sample paper is reproduced on page 85.) Although there are significant time constraints, given the need to produce seven answers in the space of about 60 minutes, candidates are nonetheless expected to adhere to the general '2 + 10 + 5' requirements across the examination as a whole. In principle, a competent Section B treatment will contain elements of description (addressing knowledge of the subject-matter), critical evaluation and commentary, third-party referencing of relevant literature and research sources, and application examples from the candidate's own work experience or from (preferably named) other organisations. Not all Section B questions lend themselves to this recipe design, yet nonetheless it is a formula that should be borne in mind both within the examination and also during all pre-examination rehearsals.

From an administrative point of view, each Section B answer is marked out of 20, with a formal allocation of marks within that figure for questions that have two or three parts. (This ensures that if students fail to address any sub-question, they automatically sacrifice a proportion of the marks available.)

A review of the entries for May 2004 has revealed the following learning points for future candidates:

1.  Just as estate agents say, 'Location, location, location' when
    invited to list the top three factors that determine the value of a
    property, so the chief examiner has to reiterate the point that,
    'Answer the question, answer the question, answer the ques-
    tion' are the top three factors which determine the mark
    awarded. The new PDS provides an opportunity for choosing
    questions (given that candidates must select seven from the
    10 available), but even so there are too many instances where
    individuals do not directly confront the topic but write about
    something else instead. It may be argued that they have
    genuinely misunderstood what is required, but this is unlikely,
    especially in view of the detailed and meticulous question-
    review process undertaken by the CIPD in collaboration with its
    chief examiners before the examination paper is finally agreed.
    Question 4 asked about the desirability of recruiting extroverts
    for call centre roles; some evaded this point altogether but
    confined themselves to lengthy advice about the selection tech-
    niques that should be used; Question 1 focused on the benefits
    and hazards of rating scales, but several wrote instead about the
    benefits and hazards of performance appraisal.

2.  Although the general background setting for Section B was the
    arrival of 10 e-mail messages, it was not necessary to structure
    any answers as if they were themselves e-mail messages;
    indeed, the rubric specifically indicated that 'You are required to
    indicate the content of your proposed response; the method
    through which you transmit your response (by e-mail, face-to-
    face discussion, and so on) need not be specified.' Nonetheless,
    a significant proportion of entrants to the examination wasted
    valuable seconds by writing entirely gratuitous greetings ('Hi,
    Sorry for the delay in replying, I have just got back from a meet-
    ing', or 'Hi, Sorry, I meant to come and talk to you about this')
    for which no marks were available. An even more unnecessary
    instance of time-wasting is this opening sentence for a treatment
    to Question 6 (about the new employment rights that came into
    effect in April 2003): 'Thank you for your recent e-mail regard-
    ing the new employment rights that have come into effect on
    6 April 2003. Identified below are the two main rights that I
    think will effect [sic] your organisation the most.' It is essential

for students to concentrate solely on making written statements that could conceivably earn marks – superfluous greetings and vacuous introductory comments cannot do so. Nor is it necessary for simplistic definitions to be supplied for the words and phrases used in a question (in tackling Question 2, about the predictive validity of the selection interview, more than one person found it necessary to define the meaning of the term 'interview' – it is 'when a potential applicant is asked questions by one or a number of members of staff').

As with Section A, many responses are supplied without any reinforcing evidence from third-party sources – indeed, as the chief examiner has pointed out in a sequence of reports on the results of the PQS Employee Resourcing examinations, it is not apparent from many scripts that the students concerned have consulted any relevant literature or research at all, not even the CIPD textbook by Stephen Taylor. It is vital that future candidates learn the simple techniques of referencing and citation – even a straightforward acknowledgment of some third-party source will be sufficient, and much better than nothing at all.

3.  The tangible existence of complacency and corporate introspection continues to be widespread. One instance will suffice. In addressing Question 2, about the poor predictive validity associated with selection interviewing, candidates were asked to explain the continued popularity of the interview in their own organisations. One wrote: 'We continue to use it because it suits our organisational needs, it's cost-effective and our organisation is still very competitive and performance levels are maintained.' Leaving aside for a moment that the term 'cost-effective' has been used when the individual clearly means 'low cost', there is no 'thinking performer' attitude at work here, no recognition of the possibility that even if existing practices 'work' (whatever that might mean), they might nonetheless 'work' even better if their validity and reliability were properly evaluated. The prevalence of wishful thinking is widespread in organisations, of course, but that is no justification for its continued popularity among CIPD students.

4.  At the same time, many of the scripts betrayed indications of genuine acceptance for the new performance expectations

associated with the PDS, and the chief examiner is optimistic
that the overall pass rate for PR will match expectations. Some
questions in particular elicited very competent responses,
particularly Question 4 (on whether extroverts are right for call
centres), Question 5 (on e-recruitment), Question 6 (on new
employment rights), and Question 9 (on the possible existence
of a 'war for talent').

## Conclusion

In conclusion, the chief examiner believes that no entirely new
problems about student performance have come into existence, as
the PDS gets under way. Criticisms about the absence of third-
party evidence, citation of independent sources, and referencing of
research and literature, are criticisms that have been made in the
past: the only difference is that such expectations are now more
vigorously and explicitly required, and failure to comply with
them is likely to lead to a 'fail' outcome in the examination.
Equally, criticisms about complacency, uninformed stereotyping
about the practice of personnel/HR in business sectors with which
the student is unfamiliar, and the failure to portray a 'thinking
performer' attitude, are all considerations to which attention has
been drawn in chief examiner reports about Employee Resourcing
in the now-superseded Professional Qualification Scheme. Again,
the only difference is that a 'thinking performer' perspective is
absolutely crucial to assimilation of the CIPD's professional standards, so its absence now becomes a legitimate cause of a 'fail'
outcome in the examination.

# SECTION 3

## EXAMINATION PRACTICE AND FEEDBACK

# 4 EXAMINATION QUESTIONS AND FEEDBACK

## Introduction

This chapter presents examination questions and proposed solutions from:

- May 2004 examination

- November 2003 examination

- May 2003 examination – complete paper

- Further practice questions of equivalent standard.

## Guidance to candidates

### Demonstrating competence

To understand how to approach and to prepare for, and to answer, People Resourcing (PR) questions one needs to understand what the examiner is searching for in terms of the demonstration of skills, knowledge and application of intelligence, that is, the ability to apply the knowledge and skills.

To understand how CIPD examiners assess PR answer scripts one has to consider the objective of the process, which is to develop individuals to become PR professionals – that is, individuals who can operate in sometimes difficult and quickly changing business environments and who have shown themselves to be capable of meeting the exacting Performance Standards of the CIPD. In essence, examiners, after marking each script, reflect upon whether the candidate has met, in an overall sense, the standards required by the CIPD.

Examiners use a three-part assessment framework:

1   *Consideration of responses to questions in context of the CIPD vision of the HR professional as a 'business partner' and 'thinking performer'.*

Consider, for example the questions posed in Section B of the paper. Typically, the chief examiner puts questions from Section B of the PR paper in the form of a request to a PR business partner from a senior executive or line manager. The response is judged in two ways: in terms of the accuracy and relevance of the information provided and the quality, that is, applicability, of the response. Candidates are expected to frame their responses in a manner that demonstrates their knowledge and understanding of the CIPD's core and what are termed BACKUP competencies (see below). These competencies (as previously discussed at length by the chief examiner) are presented in the following bullet points:

2    *The five 'BACKUP' competencies:*

- **b**usiness orientation
- **a**pplication **c**apability
- **k**nowledge of the relevant field
- **u**nderstanding
- **p**ersuasion/**p**resentation skills.

3    *The 10 core competencies*

These can be found in Part 7 of the Introduction to the CIPD Professional Standards documentation (*The vision for the new professional standards and for the competencies*):

- personal drive and effectiveness
- people management and leadership
- business understanding
- professional and ethical behaviour
- added value result achievement
- continuing learning
- analytical and intuitive/creative thinking
- 'customer' focus
- strategic thinking
- communication, persuasion and interpersonal skills.

**Convince the examiner**

It is not good enough simply to regurgitate facts. Candidates:

- Have to convince the examiner that they can add value by interpreting information provided and even, when supported by relevant evidence or debate, to show a willingness to challenge conventional wisdom or even research findings.

- Are encouraged to add to the debate (as raised by a question) by giving examples, making statements of 'fact'. Wherever possible, statements should be reinforced by citations from appropriate third-party reference sources.

- Should be able to exhibit a well-informed understanding of the practice of HR outside their own immediate organisation and business sector, and should not be narrowly focused on ethical/legal compliance as the ultimate measure of HR performance. The PR professional should be seen as active and not passive in the role.

## Some practical considerations: before and during the examination

### Preparing to answer a case study

There is no definitive way to answer this type of question. The author can pass on 'what works for him'. Candidates can then make their own minds up as to what works for them! For 'something to work' implies that practice is essential. Individuals need to practise their skills at answering case studies within a specific time limit.

So what works for the author? Consider the following process:

1. Scan-read the whole of the case study.

2. Carefully read the questions, highlighting or underlining the parts of the question that demand an answer.

3. Reread the case study, highlighting the parts that are pertinent to answering the question(s) posed.

4. Formulate a structured response in your mind.

5.  Set aside a part of the answer book as a 'scrap' or working area. Using this area put your thoughts on paper using simple bullet-point headings, in line with the structure you have thought about. When you have completed your preparation put one single line through the work and clearly mark as *'Scrap working area – not to be marked'* or something similar.

6.  Commit your response to paper. If the question asks for a report then you must write a report that includes title page, contents page, and section headings, perhaps with numbered paragraphs and so on if this is applicable. From the examiner's viewpoint it is useful if you link the sections on the contents page with the questions posed.

7.  As described previously, reread the question and then check back that your responses do in fact answer the questions posed in the case the study.

## Time management during the examination

The examination is of two hours' duration with 10 minutes given as reading time. Time is of the essence so candidates are advised to consider a 'game plan'/examination strategy.

The examination is in two parts, Section A, a case study, and Section B, which involve candidates answering seven from a possible 10 questions. The suggestion is to give equal time to Section A and Section B. The implications are:

•   Which section should be answered first? This is a difficult question and very subjective. Experience and discussion with colleagues who assist candidates to prepare for the PR examination tend to suggest that Section A should be tackled before Section B. The reasoning is not scientific but does have certain logic. Time management is of the essence, so getting to grips with Section A, within the time allowed of one hour, forces the candidate, when moving on to Section B, to consider that there are seven tasks to be completed within a maximum time of 60 minutes. Leaving Section B until last emphasises the need to apply perhaps a more rigorous control over time allocation for each individual question.

- It is very easy to 'go over the top' and spend more than the allocated eight minutes when answering a Section B question. It is so tempting to be carried away and write an extended response to a Section B question because the subject matter is within the candidate's knowledge and/or experience/comfort zone. When this happens valuable time is thus eaten away, which should have been productively used answering other questions.

- You can allow yourself approximately eight minutes to answer each question in Section B. Having only eight minutes means that there is very little thinking time to (a) select which questions to answer and (b) to think about how to approach and answer the question. The suggestion is to scan-read the whole of Section B, ticking those questions that you believe you can readily answer; and mark those that you definitely consider to be at the bottom of your selection list, leaving those in the middle ranking. Proceed to answer the questions you have ticked within the eight minutes allowed, in the order they appear in the paper. Once you have completed these questions go on to your middle-ranked questions.

  Candidates need to practise and hone their skills, both at answering case studies and the smaller Section B-type questions.

  Do not (as previously explained by the chief examiner), when answering Section B questions, write greetings and introductions as though you were answering an e-mail (if the question was in the form of an e-mail) or end your response with some form of salutation. Simply answer the question, in a logical and factual manner, and move on to the next.

- Time pressures, especially after two hours in an examination room, also affect the quality of handwriting. Examiners are not expecting candidates to produce copperplate text; they simply wish to be able to read what candidates have written. Stylised handwriting, for example, can be very difficult to interpret, so help your examiner to help you by writing clearly and legibly. We have all experienced the rush to complete questions as time pressures build, as the apparent rate of the 'passing of time' inexorably increases as the exam progresses. Handwriting, especially, takes on a life of its own with a distinct deterioration in its legibility.

- Teachers and lecturers who assist and coach PR candidates are urged to spend tutorial time working through case studies and typical Section B-type questions. Mature candidates, especially, may not have sat for a formal examination for some time (years), so it is recommended that one mock practice examination, under examination conditions, is conducted during the course of study.

- A quality response to an examination question should include reference to relevant research. Although it is unreasonable to expect candidates to produce accurately identified research or literature sources, as if writing an academic article or, indeed, the CIPD management report, you should be aware of, for example, the basic research about high-performance working (Pfeffer 2004), the 'black box' studies by Purcell (Purcell *et al* 2003), which have been discussed elsewhere in this book, and the populist research reports that appear frequently in *People Management*. Also, from the core text for the elective – *People resourcing* by Stephen Taylor – you should be able to cite either the author or some of the authorities he identifies as the foundation for his own conclusions.

- You should always try to include/identify third-party sources to support and underpin your conclusions. Avoid vague comments along the lines of 'research shows ...'. What the respective chief examiners are after, in essence, is a growing use of evidence-based argument.

### Some general comments, to reiterate some of what has previously been said

Before attempting a question, read it thoroughly and identify the key areas that the examiner is asking you to address and thus to respond to. Answer the question asked, not the question you think has been asked! Try to make life easier for the examiner and get him/her on your side by addressing simple but practical issues. Consider, for example the use of abbreviations. When using an abbreviation for the first time in your narrative, good practice is to write the meaning in full, followed by the lettered abbreviation code.

You can then save time in the following text by simply using the abbreviation; and above all please write legibly.

Do not call solely on lessons you have learned whilst in PR classes when you answer a question. Draw upon your other studies. In this way you both widen your choice of options and also enrich an appropriate response or responses to a question. Think out of the PR box because, in the world of work, we do not compartmentalise our activities but eclectically draw upon relevant knowledge and experience which informs our thinking and leads us to offering solutions to problems.

Finally the CIPD's chief examiners require candidates to respond to the questions posed in the various examinations in a manner that is informed by current good HR practice and relevant research.

## Examination criteria

Time allowed two hours plus 10 minutes' reading time.

Candidates are required to answer Section A and seven of the 10 questions in Section B.

Equal marks are allocated to each section of the paper. Within Section B, equal marks are allocated to each question.

Questions may be answered in any order.

If a question includes reference to 'your organisation', this may be interpreted as covering any organisation with which you are familiar.

The 'case study' is not based on an actual organisation. Any similarities to a known organisation are accidental.

You are likely to fail the examination if:

1.   You fail to answer seven questions in Section B, and/or

2.   You achieve less than 40 per cent in each section.

# Sample paper:
# PDS People Resourcing examination – May 2004

## Section A: case study

*It is permissible to make assumptions by adding to the case study details given below provided the essence of the case study is neither changed nor undermined in any way by what is added.*

The ANVIL brand has long been synonymous with high-quality products, advanced engineering and high performance within the automotive industry, and has competed successfully with such leaders as BMW, the Daimler-Benz group, and Jaguar. The ANVIL group took over a moribund British car manufacturer in 1994, and six years later closed down virtually its entire production facilities; yet it has retained, and has now revitalised a product, the 'Presto', that had sold more than five million cars in more than 40 years of production. The Presto was that most British of products, but was being produced in the context of a manufacturing enterprise characterised by decades of industrial relations strife and low productivity. So one of ANVIL's priorities was the need to change working practices at the Langford plant where the Presto was being made.

Geoff Dryden, change manager at ANVIL's Langford factory in the initial stages of the overhaul, says that a revamp of the working practices there was essential. 'When we started at Langford, the legacy of the previous owners and the work culture was very much "us and them". There was a blame culture within the plant and, to be honest, people had learned to leave their brains at the gate.'

Since the start of the change programme, Langford has implemented more than 8,000 ideas from staff members. Production targets during 2002 were exceeded by more than 60 per cent and those changes have contributed to savings of more than £6.3m during the past 12 months. This is not bad for a workforce that three years ago was leaving its brain at the gate.

A new change manager, Barbara Frantini, has been brought in from the parent company in the USA to drive the programme on, and she insists that the company can evolve further. 'It is my aim to make the company more like the Presto car itself, with an energetic, youthful, fun image,' she says. 'The UK workforce, traditionally, has different ethics, ways and work values. We need to start making people identify with that new image a lot more'.

'We have come a long way, but we still have a long way to go to get that ownership and to get people to recognise that they really are part of a team, a part of the plant, and a valued part of the ANVIL group.'

You are an external people resourcing consultant recruited by Barbara Frantini in order to generate some new thinking about ways to achieve the goals she has outlined in the final two paragraphs of the above text, especially so far as people resourcing strategies and practices are concerned. Write a preliminary report for your client in which you respond to the following three requirements that Barbara has outlined in her 'terms of reference' for you.

1. Making explicit use of contemporary research evidence about the resourcing approaches used in high-performance organisations, outline the resourcing strategies which you believe would facilitate achievement of the ANVIL group's vision for the Langford factory. What barriers would you expect to encounter in gaining acceptance for and in implementing these strategies, and how could they be overcome?

2. Present reasoned proposals for recruitment and selection processes that will enable the ANVIL operation at Langford fully to realise the values summarised by Barbara Frantini.

(*You should devote approximately 50 per cent of your time to each of these two tasks.*)

## Section B

Answer SEVEN of the ten questions in this section. To communicate your answers more clearly you may use whatever methods you wish, for example diagrams, flowcharts, bullet points, so long as you provide an explanation of each.

You should assume that you have just entered your office at the start of the working day and switched on your PC. The following e-mail messages appear on the screen. You are required only to indicate the content of your response to your chosen seven messages; the method you would use in order to convey your reply is not relevant.

1. *From the manager, Accounts Department:* I'm being inundated with requests for flexible working from my people. What's the legal situation about who can make such requests and the processes I should use in responding to them?

2. *From the Head of Production:* I was at a conference yesterday and heard of an investment bank which had hitherto taken on 6 per cent of its recruits through an employee referral scheme. By increasing the profile of the scheme, the bank was able to increase this to 23 per cent and cut its recruitment costs by 60 per cent. This sounds powerful to me, and a referral scheme could be useful in my area, where turnover is quite high. What are the disadvantages, though – and how could we overcome them?

3. *From the HR Director:* As you know, we're shortly planning to increase the size of our non-specialist graduate development programme and we'll need at least 100 graduates a year. I want to keep the recruitment process as cost-effective as possible, so can I have your reasoned recommendations?

4. *From the Management Development Manager:* I'd welcome your input on something that's bothering me. When filling senior executive posts in our organisation, should we in principle seek someone who's worked for all or most of his/her career with us (a 'lifer'), or someone who's worked for a variety of organisations (a 'hopper')? What does the research evidence tell us about the respective merits of each approach, and what factors should we take into account when determining our preferences?

5. *From a friend who is HR Adviser to a contact-centre business based in Doncaster:* Please help me. Our directors are attracted by the cost-reduction opportunities of taking our business to Bangalore and Mumbai. Obviously our staff doesn't want this to happen. What arguments could

I use in order to justify remaining where we are in the UK?

6. *From a journalist for* Human Resources *magazine*: Research by the Economic & Social Research Council, in its Future of Work Programme, has demonstrated that part-time and temporary work, 'portfolio' employment, home working and self-employment are not as widespread as many people think, and indeed show no signs of increasing. We're collecting inputs on this issue: what are your views, both generally and in relation to your own organisation?

7. *From the HR Planning Manager*: I'm noticing that more of our employees want to work beyond the normal retirement age. At present they don't enjoy any employment protection rights, but is this going to change in the future? If so, how should we prepare ourselves?

8. *From the regional office of the CBI*: We're fighting to preserve the 'opt out' clause which lets employees waive their right (under the EU working time directive) to a maximum 48-hour week, because we believe that withdrawing the 'opt out' clause would damage the competitiveness of UK companies and a blanket ban on long hours would breach the rights of those who want to work longer hours. Please tell us what you think about this situation, and why.

9. *From the HR administrator*: I'm studying for my CIPD exams, and I see that the examiner for People Resourcing keeps writing about 'accountability profiles'. I can't find much in the literature to tell me what they are, how they differ from job descriptions, and why they might be preferable to job descriptions. Any guidance you can give me would be very welcome.

10. *From the Managing Director*: I see that Pizza Hut has a staff turnover of more than 50 per cent, 3M's is around 5 per cent, and ours is halfway between. Summarise for me the factors that influence 'churn' in differing businesses. What does the research evidence indicate about the criteria that we should use to determine an appropriate level of staff turnover for us in our organisation?

**END OF EXAMINATION**

# Specimen answers

## PDS People Resourcing examination – May 2004: Section A

### Preparing to answer the question

When reflecting upon the requirements of this question, you should appreciate that your output, as a candidate should be:

- a preliminary report – implies that some detail will be absent.

*Audience*

- Barbara Frantini

*Content*

- Using contemporary research evidence about resourcing strategies, propose methods which would deliver the ANVIL group's vision. Identify the barriers which may delay the delivery of the strategies.

- Propose a recruitment and selection process which would enable ANVIL's operation to fully realise the values elaborated by Frantini: '… energetic, youthfulness and fun image'.

## QA I

(Note: the page structure with separate title sheet etcetera has not been used here for reasons of space.)

**Strictly confidential**

**ANVIL at Langford**

A report into the resourcing, recruitment and selection strategies to change the work culture into that of a high performing company

Report compiled by A. R. G. Candidate

**Report foreword**

Guiding the writing of this report are three pieces of work:

1. The recent work carried out by Professor John Purcell and his team, of Bath University, entitled *Understanding the people and performance link: unlocking the black box* (CIPD report 2003).

2. The work by David Guest *et al* in his CIPD (2000) report examining the 1998 WERS (Work and Employment Relations Survey) which confirmed the link between the use of more HR practices and a range of positive outcomes, including greater employee involvement, satisfaction and commitment, productivity and better financial performance.

3. *The Sheffield Effectiveness Programme*, (Patterson *et al*, IPD, 1997). The impact of people management practices on business performance, which linked good people management practices to improved bottom line results.

[*Author's note: the above three studies, perhaps with the inclusion of Harry Scarborough* et al's *study on knowledge management and the link to business performance, are three important pieces of work from which the context and content of the notion of high-performance work has been developed, and therefore at least one of the above should be quoted when answering this and similar questions.*]

**HRM strategy**

There is a need to provide in a business framework clearly expressed goals and HRM strategies which will be employed to bring around a change in business success through changes in employee behaviour and attitude. If the 'high-performance management' approach is to be adopted, whereby the company differentiates itself through innovation and superior customer service, then the overriding HRM strategy will focus on employee commitment. Flowing from this notion of improved employee commitment will be the constructs of the HR substrategies linked to the processes of: recruitment, selection and release; work systems/practices; reward; and training and development; which when bundled together encourage the desired outcome. A Performance Management System embodies many of the previous elements and would be holistic in the bringing together into one whole the appraisal, development and reward systems. Further there will have to be a sea change in management attitude away from control to empowerment and trust. The importance of a Performance Management System is that it links business goals, objectives and strategies with everyday working by providing a framework that allows monitoring of work and development processes against agreed measures.

### Work systems

- Wherever practicable, self-managed teams, work rotation and job enrichment, should be incorporated into the work flow process.

- Significant job design will also be essential to give more autonomy (and responsibility) to staff.

### Training, education and development

There will be significant requirement for training, education and development. Training in the context of the new ways of working, development in terms of understanding what is required of individuals as members of self-managed teams and education in understanding the wider business context in which ANVIL has to profitably operate.

### Reward (remuneration) systems

The reward system should reflect and reinforce the works systems and behaviours that the company intends its employees to espouse.

- *Working in teams*: implies that the reward systems focus on the reward of teams – not individuals.

- *Management attitude*: we will be requiring the company's employees to take more responsibility and be accountable for their work; they (the employees) will make mistakes as they learn, fewer as they gain experience. Management must recognise this inevitability and not blame nor castigate individuals for taking ownership and making decisions based on logic.

The bringing together of all the above in a logical format will all help to coalesce the new way in which ANVIL wishes to manage its staff.

*Recruitment, selection and release*

See later.

## Delivering the outcomes: the role of management

The process that will deliver these high performance outcomes will demand equal attention to a communication strategy that will:

- Advise employees of the problems with the current business situation and offer them a realistic vision of the future.

- Involve employees in the design and development of the 'vision' into practical processes to move the concept into reality to start the process of embedding the new cultural norms into the organisation.

- Require a bottom-up approach involving employees in education programmes linking the realities of the business market, in which the Langford plant operates, to the need for new ways of working (greater flexibility, empowerment etc.); thus to better equip them to understand the competitive market in which the company operates. This further reinforces the new ways of working and cultural norms.

- Offer staff development, linked to acquiring competences through college-based educational programmes and work-placed training and development programmes – in essence the process of emergent change (see Bernard Burnes, *Change Management*, FT Prentice Hall).

- Ensure that management embody, espouse and champion the new ways of working; paraphrasing Peter Drucker when he says, 'ANVIL management need to walk the talk'.

- Acknowledge that quality facilitation, of the change process, will be required to assist management and employees move the process forward to achieve the (combined) goals.

## Resistance to change

Not all those who are currently employees of the Langford Plant will be willing or, in some cases able, to move forward into the new nirvana. Some, through loss of status, loss of power, ignorance or perhaps fear may not be behind the change process and may politic to derail the process.

There are a number of change management processes that can be employed to deal with these eventualities, refer to Barbara Senior, *Organisational change*, FT Prentice Hall.

- Regular communication from, and between, management and employees is key to good change management practice.

- Recognising and celebrating quick wins.

- Members from 'ready to change groups' can be transferred into groups where there is a resistance to change.

- Group confrontation or group mirroring techniques can be employed to iron out issues associated with the change.

- Understanding and empathising with those who find the change difficult and opening discussion groups will solve some of the problems.

- Supervisors will clearly have to adopt a new role. They will have to move from a supervisory into a consultant or facilitating role when the self-managed teams become operational. Some (supervisors) will be able to adopt but some will not and unfortunately they will have to leave ANVIL employment (see 'remuneration' above).

### Recruitment, selection and release

The recruitment process will also need to reflect the 'new' requirements. Not all staff will be able to cope with the increase in responsibilities they will be required to shoulder. The 'hiring bar' will, in all probability, have to be raised.

The attitude of staff is vital to high-performance working thus recognising the CIPD mantra of recruit for attitude and train for skill.

The employment decision is a two-way process. Candidates can either choose to join the company or choose not to join. Consequently there is a need to give prospective employees sufficient information to make that vital decision as to whether they feel/believe that prospective employment with ANVIL will meet with their aspirations for work and whether the work systems meet their personal needs for fulfilment.

It is therefore proposed that ANVIL:

- Moves away from job descriptions to *accountability profiles* thus focusing the need to recruit staff who are flexible and adaptable to change. In this way the implied notion that: 'we are searching for staff who can manage within a changing environment' becomes explicit.

- Use *assessment centres coupled with psychological/psychometric testing* focusing on specific personality traits (for example, good interpersonal skills, temperament) and a flexibility of perspective coupled with the ability to adapt to changing circumstance.

- Develop structured selection days involving *work experience* for potential employees.

- Consider a *graduate recruitment* and selection programme based upon close liaison with local universities and summer work experience programmes for undergraduates.

- Recognise that internally there is a need to identify and manage the talent which already exists within the organisation, to consider the need to succession plan by giving those with the appropriate attitude and potential chance to experience new roles, attain new skills and be challenged in their work.

- In matters of *team selection*: when recruiting individuals to join self-managed teams, include members of these teams as part of the selection process; because new team members will have to quickly become part of a close knit and self-reliant group.

- *Develop an induction process*: this process will need to be thoroughly thought through and developed to address not only the immediate needs of the job but the wider understanding of the plant in its business environment.

### Release from the organisation

- Not all who are currently working in the organisation will have a place in the new operation; there may simply be no job for them or perhaps, because their role has changed, they will not be able to adapt and adopt new ways of working. Good quality redundancy/severance schemes, involving support and professional 'outplacement' guidance with job searching and preparing for a new world outside will be a necessary appendage to the short-term activities while ANVIL is moving forward.

• We must also recognise that the staff that are left in the organisation, the survivors, will need support over this interim period.

## Conclusions

The key to future success is having a clear vision of what is required, involving staff in the development of this vision and then communicating the agreed vision and how it is to be implemented to all.

Culture change has to be a bottom-up approach but wholeheartedly supported by management. It encompasses all the HR processes so they must be designed to reinforce the overall desired outcome.

The change will take time and there will be a requirement to 'check back, to test' with our employees to determine that 'we' are not slipping back to 'us' and 'them'.

# Specimen answers

## PDS People Resourcing examination – May 2004: Section B

Each Section B question is marked out of 20 possible marks and candidates have to make a credible attempt at each of the seven questions they are required to answer.

### Question I

*[Author's note: See page 85 for the questions. Answers to this type of question should include:*

- *Applicable legislative instrument (for example, Employment Act 2002).*

- *Coverage – to whom does it apply? (which employee groups and which type of businesses – for example some legislation may not apply to small business, that is, those with < 20 employees).*

- *What does the legislation say and how does it impact upon employer and employee?*

- *Special limitations (for example, time windows for application and for management responses).*

- *Appeals procedure.*

*Bearing the above in mind the proposed answer to the question is as below.]*

The Employment Act 2002 is the relevant legislative instrument that applies to this question. The important points to remember (and of course which constitute good practice) are:

- Staff who have completed 26 weeks service and the parent of a child aged less than six years or under 18 years if disabled.

- Applications must be in writing and only one may be made within a 12-month period.

- Management has 28 days in which to consider the application and to reply, in writing, to the request either agreeing to or refusing the request. Requests must be addressed by management in a genuine manner. Good practice would probably involve discussion with others who would be affected by the request, perhaps resulting in workable compromises.

- Requests can be refused on a number of grounds: burden of extra cost, productivity problems, an inability to reorganise the work, and inability to recruit extra staff. Business should consider the applications with a positive and open-minded attitude and response in the spirit in which the legislation was developed.

- Staff who have had their applications refused have redress to the normal grievance procedures and finally through the Employment Tribunal System should the procedures not have been followed correctly.

Management/supervisory staff should be trained in dealing with these types of requests and understand the relevant legislation. A company's approach to flexible working goes further than simply agreeing to individual requests. It is about work/life balance and is part of the total approach to employee resourcing against which staff measures the firm and thus impacts upon the commitment equation. (Refer to the CIPD's *How to guide on flexible working* for further detail).

---

### Student response to Question 1 (as written)

Employees with children under 6 and 18, if disabled, have the right to make a request for flexible working.

- The request must be in writing.

- The request must be responded to within 28 days and a meeting with the employee arranged. The employee can be accompanied by a fellow employee to the meeting

- Within 14 days of the meeting of the employer must reply in writing either agreeing or refusing the request. If the request is refused the reasons must be outlined i.e. extra cost to the business, not enough staff to cover the change in working pattern.

- The employee has 14 days from receipt of the letter to make an appeal.

'Name of firm specified' have implemented a flexible working environment with only 3 per cent of their workforce not taking advantage of it.

### Author's assessment of the candidate's response

The examiner awarded 12 marks for this attempt and therefore this question was graded (individually) as a pass. Roughly a quarter of the marks would be allocated to defining the legislative detail, with the remainder of the marks to the process and business issues addressed.

'Standing back' from the question posed, what should we, as HR professionals, consider when we give our response? The guidance given on page 00 in my model answer puts a framework around the response and gives it the 'M'-level quality.

In essence, to whom does the legislation apply? What impact does this (request) have on the business, and what scope does the manager have to work within? What would be regarded as a reasonable response? What are the process factors which the manager has to observe?

*What did the candidate do right?* He/she answered the question that was asked, which was to give advice about the legal situation in respect of flexible working requests. Those who can apply were correctly identified and some detail of the process requirements was given.

*What did the candidate do wrong; where could the extra marks be picked up?* She/he did not say which legislative instrument applies – this is the essential underpinning. It also gives authority to the response. The candidate did not give sufficient detail about the scope within which the manager can assess the request, in terms of impact upon production/working, co-workers and the link between such requests and the company's overall perspective on work life balance.

## Question 2

This question refers to the recruitment of staff by personal referral from existing employees of the company. There are positive and negative aspects of employing this mechanism. Should the option be seriously considered then there has to be some form of formal mechanism within which it operates. The process should be:

- Transparent.

- Detail in simple terms how staff nominate friends and associates.

- State what is in it for staff that make nominations.

- State what type of 'bounty' is paid and when – on recruitment of the individual, after six months of working? (It is probably better to keep this part of the process simple and not to include too many caveats.)

This option provides a viable alternative to the traditional methods of recruitment, especially when labour markets are tight or if the firm is trying to gain access into specific labour markets, for example ethnic groups.

As previously mentioned, there are 'downs' as well as 'ups' with the process.

Nepotism is an issue as well as the likelihood of recruiting from and into the same mould. There is also the potential for the formation of exclusive cliques, ethnic and other groups that can negatively impact upon working relationships and cause discrimination in an otherwise fair recruitment and selection mechanism. Diversity can suffer leading to a bland population with few individuals who challenge the norms and enliven the business.

However, once the strengths and weaknesses of the process have been recognised, the negative impact can be mitigated by monitoring for discriminatory practices/unequal treatment of groups. The referral option is but one weapon in the armoury of the professional recruiter.

## Question 3

Stephen Taylor has a relevant section on this issue in his *People resourcing* text. It is also worth reviewing what the Association of Graduate Recruiters and the 'Prospects' (government-sponsored) 'official' graduate website has to say on the subject, although the AGR's website applicability is limited for non-members.

Many (high-profile) companies operate their own website. The quality of the website is all-important. It should give sufficient information about the firm to enable potential recruits to decide whether they wish to continue with the recruitment process. Most sites also include some form of self-administered pre-recruitment assessment test. This is expected and also good practice.

Other options that make sense include linking with a limited number of universities that have a track record of supplying quality graduates. A number of firms also offer focused graduate training programmes and summer tasters (work experience) prior to graduation, for instance, Waitrose and Tesco. As Stephen Taylor says, one way is to generally lift the profile of the firm by liaising with universities and schools, assisting with projects and, as previously mentioned, offering work experience. The government, in its bid to entice mathematics and science graduates into schools, has considered both the mechanisms for attracting graduates to train: in the short term in the form of training bursaries and golden hellos, and in the long term by improving the salary prospects of graduate mathematics and science teachers.

Once it is recognised that there is a cost to the recruitment and selection activity, there is a need to review the various options that lead to successful recruitment by a post-activity cost–benefit analysis of the options employed, perhaps coupled with some form of benchmarking exercise. Measuring the relative cost and effectiveness of different methods is not just logical but essential.

### Student response to Question 3 (as written)

The Internet is reported in the *Guide to Recruitment Consultants,* (April 2004) as an effective means of attracting graduates. The cost starts around 6k for 12 months available 24/7 compared with advertising in a national paper @ 7k. The advantages of the Internet are that the recruitment net is widened and more candidates can self-select.

### Author's assessment of the candidate's response

The examiner awarded nine marks for this question. It is a 'credible attempt' at 45 per cent of the available marks but, when measured on an individual basis, would be a fail.

*What did the candidate do right?* The question focused on cost-effective solutions to the process of non-specialist graduate recruitment and, quite rightly, the candidate introduced evidence against which he/she has made recommendations, giving the availability and cost advantages and disadvantages of two forms of advertising. The candidate also recognised that there is a need to give sufficient information about the company and its activities so that applicants are able to self determine whether or not they wished to proceed with the application process.

*What did the candidate do wrong?* Graduate recruitment is not a 'run of the mill' activity. There is a certain gravitas about it because of the long-term implications of getting it right (or wrong). Cost-effectiveness was the theme that the HR director introduced through his/her question on graduate recruitment. Graduate recruitment is a process and therefore it is the effectiveness of the overall process that should be considered and therefore measured and benchmarked.

The recruitment process is divergent; the objective of it is to attract as many graduates with the appropriate knowledge skills and attributes as possible. The question states that there is a need for 100+ graduates a year. There will, therefore, be a need for a number of alternative approaches to the recruitment exercise, thus the model response suggests the Internet as well as a relational approach, as advocated by Taylor. Once the peak of recruitment has been reached, the relational approach would be the main source of student feedstock. It is worth recognising that companies that have a recognised brand image are increasingly taking advantage of this and recruiting directly from their own website at marginal extra cost.

[*Author's supplementary note*: although not asked for in this question, there are of course other special cases; for example, in the case of graduate recruitment for a blue-chip company with a world presence. In this situation the graduate recruitment activity would reflect its worldwide presence. This is easily accomplished using the Internet, which in turn would be further supplemented and enhanced by the forging of links with universities in the various host countries in which the company operates.]

## Question 4

In respect to the preference between home-grown talent or talent which has had a wide variety of experience there are clear advantages and disadvantages between the two options.

For those companies like ours, which has embraced new technology and new ways of working and recognised that knowledge management is more than holding information on data bases and is fundamental to the process of innovation, we have to ask ourselves how much is the tacit knowledge which forms every part of our business life and which cannot be taught, but is hard gained through years of experience within the one business, vital to our top management? Having processes, supported by HR strategies, which positively encourage the socialising of knowledge, teamworking, mentoring, sharing knowledge and so on (see John Storey 2001 – a critical text – and also Harry Scarborough and Chris Carter's review of the key knowledge management in *Investigating knowledge management*) mitigate the need to look outside for talent at these levels. Should we not have these mechanisms in place then there is a need to consider the advantages of recruiting into the business senior management who have a broad church of experience and who can enrich the organisation by:

- engendering a diversity of approach by introducing new ways of thinking, new perspectives on problem solving and new ways of working
- upsetting, disturbing, de-stabilising and challenging the status quo.

## Question 5

[*Author's note*: many companies have benefited from offshoring their call centre activities but some have pulled back from such overseas outsourcing. On the positive side of the equation labour costs are cheaper in countries like India and staff are well qualified and, relative for the location, well paid. There have been some notable success stories: the Prudential for example, has a wholly owned company in Mumbai in which its call centre staff are fully inculcated in the business and thus live the brand. The question, though, asks for a one-sided view.]

There are a number of issues that can impact negatively upon the operation of the call centre. Staff turnover can be high (*circa* 35 per cent) as trained staff (competent English speakers) move from job to job to obtain better pay deals. Embedding the brand and getting overseas staff to live/understand what the brand means can be difficult because of the cultural differences and a lack of understanding of the reputation of the brand in the United Kingdom. A number of companies have pulled away from deals. Dell for example, in the United States, has pulled back its call centre staff because of the lack of employer commitment. Dell, though, had outsourced its call centre to a generic provider and had not developed a subsidiary in India. Practical considerations such as political stability and guaranteed availability of utility services (electricity, water) can be a problem. There is also the issue that many customers do not like their bank accounts and so on (research by the Alliance and Leicester) handled by staff overseas. The perception by customers about how the brand has been managed, should their queries have been poorly handled, creates a disproportionately jaundiced view if the transaction was with staff in an overseas call centre.

Offshoring is not a simple process of finding a possible provider and then handing over the service. There is a need for a more profound and deeper review as to why the process should be contracted out offshore and the long-term implications of taking such action.

## Question 6

Since David Guest's first proposition in the mid-1980s when he linked flexible working with high-commitment practices and Atkinson published his model of the flexible firm, research has shown (Cully *et al* 1998; WERS Survey) that flexible working has not been approached from a strategic perspective by business but rather addressed in an ad hoc manner. Business has responded to individual requests rather than assessing the needs systematically and strategically.

In medium to large firms part-time working, (non-standard working) especially for females, has increased but other forms have remained static. From the employees' perspective they perceive that the opportunity to work flexibly is very much occupation-specific: clerical or cleaning rather than operative and assembly work.

In small businesses (10–99 employees) the incidence of non-standard working was significant.

With a tight labour market in the United Kingdom there will be a need to think more radically and strategically about flexible working in order to attract and retain staff.

From the perspective of our business we see significant advantages in promoting flexible and non-standard working and so we are going to take a leaf out of Barclays' book:

Barclays wanted to maximise its ability to attract and retain staff, so it:

- reviewed its retirement and recruitment policies

- considered the implications of age diversity across their business

- announced rights to request flexible work

- reviewed all HR policies to ensure no age bias

- gave staff the right to work until the age of 65

- raised age diversity awareness levels

- identified factors that were an issue for different age groups.

We are currently reviewing how we do business with a view to assessing how and where flexible/non-standard working practices best fit our operations.

## Question 7

Currently there is a debate running about this very subject: see the government's Age Positive Campaign website and CBI website for relevant comment. The Department for Work and Pensions (DWP) considers that the mandatory retirement age should be thrown into the 'dustbin of social history'. It considers that to release a productive member of staff through retirement makes no sense. Firms are debating whether there should be an enforceable retirement age and as such are stalling the publication of the relevant draft age discrimination legislation, due for implementation in 2006. Legislation is planned to appear in 2006 but there are two camps of thought:

- There is a strong argument for a default retirement age for an interim period to help employers adjust. This stance is supported by the business through the CBI and the EEF (Engineering Employers Federation). They are concerned over unfair or wrongful dismissal litigation by older employees and the associated tribunal costs. Without mandatory retirement employers would have to make people redundant or 'performance manage' them out of an organisation.

- The CIPD's stance is that the mandatory retirement age should be abolished. They also reject the proposal for a default retirement age.

Interestingly companies like B&Q support wholeheartedly the CIPD stance, pointing out that the older worker makes a valid contribution to their business.

In short, therefore, it will be prudent to prepare for the introduction of such legislation.

In response to the probable introduction of this type of legislation the business would have to review:

- Its retirement and pension policies.

- Its recruitment strategies, literature and training to reflect the requirement to be age neutral.

- Its processes for dealing with poor/lack of performance of older employees yet recognising their contribution to the business. Perhaps cash incentives to retire or enhancements to pension. Using the poor performance procedure is always an option.

## Question 8

[*Author's note*: the examiner is using the originator of the e-mail here in two ways. The first way is very simple and is to introduce the question. The second is to introduce a perspective into the question, which is subtle and designed to test awareness of the candidate to the possibility of polarisation of debate and view. The chief examiner introduces the question in the context of the perspective the CBI has adopted, as an employers' organisation which has a self-evident 'right-leaning' employer interest in the outcomes of the debate. Your answers should, therefore, reflect awareness of this perspective.]

Currently the majority of those who work long hours, over the 48 hours per week quoted in the e-mail, do so, not because they are forced to work extra hours but because they see the need to work extra hours to complete outstanding work or alternatively to earn overtime payments to improve their standard of living. Employees generally are in favour of the 'opt out clause' which allows them to work extra time, while at the same time they recognise that it can and does damage both their psychological and physical health.

Employers see the removal of the 'opt out clause' as a reduction in the options available for flexible working. Working long hours is not a motivator and can quickly become a demotivator if there is a constant requirement for this type of working. Working longer does not necessarily equate to working efficiently or effectively. The issue is how to improve corporate productivity without the negative impact, which a long-hours culture engenders. Motivation theory suggests giving staff more autonomy and improving the options for flexible working.

In reality there will be a balance between the 35-hour week that the French government introduced (to increase employment?) and perhaps will repeal in the not too distant future, and the 48-hour 'opt out clause' on which we in the United Kingdom are fighting a rearguard action.

The CIPD's view is clear and in favour of scrapping the 48-hour 'opt-out' clause. It is about the balance between work and life and arguably enjoying both.

---

### Student response to Question 8 (as written)

I think that the 'opt out' clause should go. It will make for a healthier workforce with a proper work life balance and will allow recourse by employees on *employers who hold a 'gun' at their heads* that do not sign up for an opt out (eg they are paid off). A work force that works fewer hours will produce more opportunities for employment. *Re employment trends (Workforce Employee Relations Survey 1998)* so that job share, part time working, career breaks are all increasing.

The French have a *statutory 35-hour working week and are managing to keep up with the rest of the European states* in terms of employment and productivity.

### Author's assessment of the candidate's response

For the above response the candidate was awarded six marks and therefore was classed as a fail (on an individual basis). The marks were awarded for the ideas, which he/she has expressed in the comments highlighted in the above answer. Credit has been given for quoting from recognised sources, in this case the WERS survey of 1998, and having an awareness of actions that partner governments (in the EU) have adopted.

The analysis could have been improved by considering both the moral and ethical issues of the demands placed on the employee, whether of his/her free will or by some form of coercion, for work (time) over and above that which would be considered reasonable and concomitant with the maintenance of a balance between work and life. The other consideration is the business case:

- Does working longer hours lead to greater productivity?

- What is the impact upon the health of employees who regularly engage in long-hours working?

- What is the impact upon morale and commitment?

Research by people like John Purcell *et al* (2003) in *Unlocking the black box* and Frederick Herzberg in his famous paper of 1968 on motivation published in the *Harvard Business Review* ('One more time: how do you motivate employees') demonstrate that it is the way we manage people that counts (Herzberg with his 'extrinsic/intrinsic motivators' and Purcell demonstrating the link between how we manage people and the 'bottom line'), and working longer hours does not necessarily equate to effective working. The WERS survey recognises that working long hours has a detrimental effect on the health of employees. Should an employee's illness be linked to a work-related condition (stress, for example), the employer is in contravention of the Health and Safety at Work Act 1974.

The advice, which is what we have been asked to provide (by the CBI), should be based upon the above research-driven outcomes.

[*Further comment by the author:* we all have to work long hours from time to time to meet deadlines. The above question is about the regular working of long hours, week on week, over and above the recommended 48 hours maximum per week. Although the above analysis is long-winded and would therefore not be presented as a recommended response per se, it does give some idea how to analyse the problem and thus formulate your response.]

## Question 9

Although I agree in general with your comment that there is little information about 'accountability profiles', they are addressed in both Stephen Taylor's *People resourcing* and Mick Marchington and Adrian Wilkinson's *People management and development: human resource management at work.*

As Marchington and Wilkinson say, job descriptions have been subject to criticism, being outmoded and irrelevant to modern conditions and more relevant to a rule-oriented culture. Accountability profiles are less specific than job descriptions, usually no more than one page in length, and as their name implies, concerned with the job outcomes; that is what the individual is responsible and accountable to deliver. They purposefully focus on key performance areas. The accountability profile is purposefully kept vague because the idea is to encourage staff to engage in discretionary behaviour; to go beyond contract.

Accountability or job profiles are not intrinsically a nirvana because they too have problems. As Taylor points out, going back to the well-worn and much-abused job description/role profile, it can be said that it does have its uses especially in the arena of poor performance. Engaging staff against a very 'broad ranging and loose' accountability profile does not give potential recruits a picture of the organisation and their workplace, and so trouble is potentially stored for the future.

That said, the accountability profile has gained much favour. Management can with greater clarity consider the need or worth of roles, because they do not have to wade through detailed job descriptions, and therefore can make better quality HR planning decisions. Incorporating accountability profiles with four or five core competencies, based on behavioural traits, is perhaps a way ahead. (Specific departments may have some key functional competencies which they would wish to add.)

## Question 10    *turnover*

A good place to start when considering the relativities of labour turnover rates is the CIPD's annual survey that provides the rates analysed by industry sector and by occupation. The data is also sorted (categorised) by voluntary or other sector.

At the low end (of the turnover statistics) sit the utilities (electricity, gas and water at just under 9 per cent), while at the high end are the call centre sector (*circa* 50 per cent) and hotel, catering and leisure (*circa* 45 per cent) with the remainder 20 per cent or below, and many around the 12 per cent level.

Typically, sectors that employ part-time or workers in other forms of temporary roles (let us call it flexible work practice but with no employee long-term commitment) there is an expectation that turnover will be significant. Pizza Hut is characteristic of this latter sector, with part-time roles predominantly occupied by young people.

There is an optimum turnover rate; a balance between too low (perhaps at less than 5 per cent) and too high (above 15 per cent). Too low a staff turnover does not provide the opportunity to enliven the organisation with new talent (see Stephen Taylor, *People resourcing*). The rate can be too high when recruitment costs can vary from the average cost of *circa* £5,000 (*CIPD resourcing survey 2004*) but this clearly depends upon the level of staff involved, whether the position is advertised nationally or perhaps headhunters are engaged, thus escalating costs, and the type of selection method employed, interview or assessment centre). This of course does not include the loss of business caused by the time to resource (typically three months + or −) and the time it takes for the individual to 'get up to speed' – which once again is a function of the level of the position resourced in the organisation.

The focus needs to be on the key roles, the knowledge workers: those who by the nature of the job hold the tacit and core knowledge of the business. It is about knowledge management.

In the 2004 report on Recruitment, retention and turnover, the CIPD has identified that the major four reasons for leaving an organisation are: promotion outside, change of career, level of pay and lack of development or career opportunities The quality of communication (this goes back to Henry Mintzberg's work of the mid-1970s) is a vital component of the commitment equation, which of course links with quality leadership and how people are managed (refer to the Purcell *et al* 2003, *Understanding the people–performance link: unlocking the black box*, CIPD).

# Sample paper:
# PDS People Resourcing examination –
# November 2003

## Section A: case study

*It is permissible to make assumptions by adding to the case study details given below provided the essence of the case study is neither changed nor undermined in any way by what is added.*

You are an internal Human Resources (HR) consultant within a local authority that now wishes to recruit an outsourcing provider to supply some key support roles, such as customer-facing services and related back-office processes, including those within the HR function itself. It is envisaged that the contract, when awarded, will run for 15 years with break clauses at the end of the fifth and tenth years.

You have been asked to prepare a report for the chief executive (CEO) and the management team in which you deal with the feasibility of an outsourcing strategy, the possible problems and how to overcome them, and an action programme for the recruitment and selection of an effective outsourcing partner. In preparing for the report, you have investigated what is known about the experience of outsourcing, and have discovered that:

1. Several other local authorities, like Lambeth and Westminster, have opted for what is known as business-process outsourcing (BPO), with companies such as Capita and Vertex. Liverpool Council, by contrast, has decided to go down the partnership route by creating a joint-venture company with British Telecommunications plc (BT) to which some 800 staff have been seconded (secondment being a way of avoiding the implications of Transfer of Undertakings (Protection of Employment) (TUPE) and thus enabling staff to focus their energies on improving the business, it is claimed). Kent County Council has rejected outsourcing altogether, arguing that the business case is at best marginal and the strategic loss of control is too dangerous.

2. Hertfordshire County Council (HCC) employed Manpower in 2000 to fill 10,000 full-time vacancies and cut administrative costs, while significantly reducing the overall management time devoted to recruitment. Manpower now claims it is on target to reduce HCC's recruitment budget by 5 per cent. Along similar lines, Capita routinely claims it can save between 15 and 25 per cent of the original cost of delivery of services when acting on behalf of its public sector clients, and it can simultaneously improve service levels.

3. A senior officer for one of the central London boroughs emphasises that 'it is absolutely clear what you are going to get and how.' It is possible to be taken in by sales teams who 'can promise the earth for a fantastic price', but who are not the people who have to deliver. When things go wrong, invoking penalties does not help, either, because 'slapping on penalties leads you down a path that is almost impossible to get back from. You need both parties to work together to agree a clear improvement plan.'

4. Problems with the housing benefit service at Lambeth were exacerbated by Capita's reluctance to take on extra staff to cope with exceptional difficulties. In the words of a senior Lambeth official, 'this is one of the lessons that we learnt about dealing with the private sector: if you get someone coming in underbidding, you get an "under service" as a result.' The Audit Commission has criticised Lambeth for not managing the contract properly, for allowing the situation to get out of hand, and for not issuing a single default notice during the four years that Capita has held the contract.

On the basis of the above information, supplemented by your own judgments, produce the report that your CEO and her management team have requested. Wherever possible you should reinforce your material with references to published case studies, research and other third-party sources. You should focus on each of these three specific questions:

1. Briefly examine and evaluate the evidence about the benefits and risks associated with outsourcing.

2. Design a systematic approach for the recruitment and selection of effective outsourcing providers for your local authority.

3. Outline and justify the principles that should underpin the relationship between your local authority and its chosen outsourcing provider.

(*You should devote approximately equal amounts of time to each of the three issues.*)

## Section B

Answer SEVEN of the ten questions in this section. To communicate your answers more clearly you may use whatever methods you wish, for example diagrams, flowcharts, bullet points, so long as you provide an explanation of each.

You should assume that you have just entered your office at the start of the working day and switched on your PC. The following e-mail messages appear on the screen. You are required only to indicate the content of your response; the method you would use in order to convey your reply is not relevant.

1. *From one of your Human Resource (HR) team members*: We're relying more and more on recruitment agencies for some of our key call-centre and IT jobs, and what I'm finding, in essence, is that the agency is trying to find jobs for people, whereas we're trying to find people for jobs. The two don't fit together. What can we do to make the agency work more effectively for us?

2. *From two business unit managers*: We're both very short of competent people to lead a couple of big projects, and we've heard about a thing called "interim management" which perhaps could help us. Can you explain what it's about, and summarise the pros and cons of using 'interim managers'?

3. *From the HR Planning executive:* I just saw an article in *People Management* claiming that 'there are compelling business and legal reasons' why organisations need to take the issue

of ageism seriously. I must have missed this – so can you summarise the evidence for me, and suggest what we should be doing about it?

4. *From the HR director*: When I was at last year's CIPD National Conference, I heard that some organisations have responded to the so-called 'war for talent' by creating special positions, e.g., America On Line has a 'talent acquisition department' and media group WPP has a 'chief talent officer'. What is the evidence for and against us doing something similar?

5. *From a close personal friend who is HR Manager at a supermarket company:* Please help me. My company is much smaller than the other supermarket firms in the UK; our share price has fallen; we've been making people redundant as we dispose of less profitable stores. It is notoriously difficult to recruit and retain staff in retailing, and we can't offer the high-base salaries that Tesco and Sainsbury's give their people. What can we learn from the recent research about how to optimise people performance and commitment?

6. *From a* People Management *journalist*: We're preparing a feature for our next issue. Can we have your views on the links between corporate ethicality, employer branding and people resourcing, both in general and also so far as your own organisation is concerned?

7. *From the Company Secretary*: I was glancing through *People Management* yesterday and saw a brief comment that 'In an ideal world, rogue employees would be weeded out during recruitment'. How can we ensure this is done?

8. *From the Operations Manager*: I've just been approached to give a reference about one of my former employees. I've never done this before, so can you give me some 'do's' and 'don'ts', please?

9. *From the International Marketing Manager:* We're just about to recruit some people for our growing operation overseas (mainly in Africa and Asia–Pacific), and we need to get it right because out there they'll be on their own. What does research tell us about the personality and other attributes that are valuable predictors of success in expatriate roles?

10. *From the Research and Development Manager*: Some HR people are keen on competency frameworks, but the CIPD's own document, *Managing Learning for Added Value*, says that they 'can come across as unrealistic specifications for "paragons of virtue on a good day", or as meaningless to those who are expected to use them to inform their decisions.' What do you think? If competency frameworks are the way forward, how can they be made to work?

**END OF EXAMINATION**

# Specimen answers

## PDS People Resourcing examination – November 2003: Section A

### Preparing to answer the question

When answering this type of case study question candidates should reflect upon what the examiner wishes to see, in terms of a response. Underline or highlight the key phrases and paragraphs. In this case the output is a *report for the chief executive officer and management team of the local authority*. The report must contain *discussion of the feasibility of an outsourcing strategy, possible problems, solutions and an action programme for recruitment and selection* of an effective outsourcing partner. If your response does not contain all these elements, you have immediately reduced your possible marks.

Although time-consuming, it is good practice to have prepared by writing a number of reports in response to previous past papers. In doing this you will embed in your mind what is required in respect of format/structure, thus allowing you to focus purely on content. Spend a few minutes structuring your response on a clean page of the answer book, plotting the format and the key headings you need to address. When you have completed your plan put a neat line through the work, and clearly and neatly write 'Please do not mark – rough work' or something similar. Then follow your plan.

# QA I

## Stokeshire County Council

A Report into the feasibility of outsourcing: payroll, recruitment and associated personnel administration activities and HR Intranet Systems.

A report compiled by A. R. G. Candidate

**Contents of Section A**

Note: the page numbers refer to pages in the report not this guide.

## A. Benefits and risks of outsourcing activities

From a business perspective there has to be clarity of understanding why outsourcing is being considered. In Stokeshire's case, initial studies show that:

- Payroll, recruitment and associated personnel administration activities and HR intranet systems can be considered as non-core to the HR business and with appropriate controls can safely be contracted out.

- There is a costed benefit based upon the outsource agent

providing the staff and related IT systems to manage the payroll and recruitment processes. In essence our back-office activity becomes the front-office activity of the outsource agent. (Taylor pp 421–9) discusses these issues in some depth.

• The council's HR staff can focus upon the strategic activities of business improvement without becoming bogged down in some of the minutiae of managing the day-to-day activities of the recruitment and payroll processes.

The success of outsourcing these activities will be:

• In the contractual detail (see later, there is always concern about losing control of the process). Preparing to contract out, thinking about what is to be contracted out, for how long and how this will be effectively managed, while maintaining an arms' length control of the process with appropriate checks and balances built in (reporting requirements, meetings and so on) will be a vital component of the contractual and business arrangement.

• In selecting a partner that has a similar or compatible business ethos to that of the council.

• Recognising that the relationship between the outsourcing provider and the council will have to be positively managed by the council's HR staff; this implies trained staff that are competent in contract management. In this respect we (Stokeshire) will have to draw upon help and guidance from the 'legal and contracts' and 'computing' departments of the council who have significant experience in the management of outsourcing contractors. Our staff are able but not yet trained and are not experienced in the process of contract management.

Further issues associated with the outsourcing process can be found in *People Management* (13 June 2002).

### B. Recruiting and selection of the outsourcing provider

(See later for detailed action plan/timescale.)

The process that is recommended is similar to the process one would use when recruiting and selecting staff but with a few additions. Listed below are some of the critical stages:

1.  Identification of possible candidate organisations: contact CIPD, sister councils, private organisations for assistance in identifying competent providers.

2.  Prepare the tender document:

    i.   Define in detail the activities (scope of work) of both the outsource agent and the council's HR specialist who will be the contract manager.

    ii.  Define the controls, in terms of reports, meetings, roles and responsibilities, of the provider and council contract manager.

    iii. Define the person specification of key outsource agent staff that would be involved in the work. (Outsource agents would be expected to provide CVs of prospective *staff who would be assigned to the project – not just CVs of type!*).

    iv.  Define due diligence requirements, such as: (a) What experience have the respective organisations had of these activities? (b) How long have they been in the business? (c) Who have they in their current client portfolio (possibility to visit current clients)? (d) Do they have performance management systems in place for their own staff? [*Author's comment*: Here you are demonstrating that you have an understanding of the business by asking some basic questions that would indicate the professional credentials of prospective partners.]

    v.   Define the structure financial/remuneration package.

    vi.  Scope out a balanced scorecard against which pre-qualification of candidate organisations takes place.

         [*Author's comment*: Here you are demonstrating that you appreciate that the lowest tender is not always the best tender because there are other (soft) factors which impact upon business success and which would not be considered if the choice is made purely on cost factors. It is better to put these 'upfront' rather than try to convince senior management of their import once they have seen attractive figures from the cheaper (cheerful) sector of the outsourcing business.]

3.  Tender documents, minus the financial structure of the tender, (Invitation to pre-qualify) are despatched and firms are invited to a clarification meeting at the council offices.

    (*Note*: the tender document will form the basis of the legal contract between the two parties once the selection process is completed.)

4.  A pre-qualification process that involves reviewing the responses to the initial tender document against the criteria specified in the balanced scorecard. A short list (of three outsource agents) will be developed after a desktop review of the invitation to tender documents by HR senior management. An onsite visit to the short-listed outsource agents together with follow-up visits to (a selection) of their current clients.

5.  Successful outsource agents that have pre-qualified are requested to complete the financial element of the invitation to tender and are subsequently invited to make a presentation and respond to a Q&A session with the CEO, senior HR, IT and legal/contracts staff of Stokeshire council.

6.  A decision is made on the preceding documentation and presentations against a pre-prepared scorecard.

## C. Principles of the business relationship

The development of a positive relationship is key to the success of the outsourcing activity. In any business relationship there has to be recognition that the client requires a quality service and the service provider is there to make a profit. In this type of arrangement the relationship should be symbiotic (one needs the other to survive) and built upon trust. It should be tempered with a recognition that there is a requirement, on both sides, to work within a business framework that requires the outsource agent to demonstrate integrity, through the provision of a quality service both in spirit and deed, supported by hard business data, and requires the client (in this case Stokeshire Council) to manage both within an agreed regulatory framework and in the spirit of the agreement. As with the tender, and thus the final contractual agreement, the devil is in the detail. The outsource agent's key management and supervisory staff should be:

- Inducted into the business culture of the council as a matter of normal process.

- Required to attend, as detailed within the contract's framework, regular (documented) meetings that cover the key Performance Indicators and other business issues. The meetings themselves will be important to the effective management of the contract, and the minutes provide a formal trail of activity for audit purposes.

The council's nominated HR service contract manager should develop and nurture a mutual understanding between him/herself and the outsource agent.

### D. Action plan

Commencing from week zero:

| Activity | Responsible Stokeshire party/activity | Time |
|---|---|---|
| Identify outsourcing providers | HR business partner | 4 weeks (part-time activity) |
| 1. Develop tender and cost model for the outsourcing activity.<br>2. Produce list of companies eligible for pre-qualification exercise. | HR business + (advice from sister councils), internal: contracts and legal dept., IT dept. – lots of experience with outsourcing | 4 weeks (in parallel with the above) |
| Gain approval for tender exercise and companies who will be invited to pre-qualify | HR business partner, HR director, tender board (contracts and legal) | 1 week |
| Dispatch invitation to tender | HR business partner | With above 2/3 weeks |

| Activity | Responsible Stokeshire party/activity | Time |
|---|---|---|
| Clarification of queries, points and ambiguities from companies. Visit possible outsourcing service providers and their current clients | HR business partner | 2 weeks |
| Select those who have pre-qualified (final short-list) and invite formal financial tender | HR business partner, HR director | 2 weeks |
| Make final selection (from prepared scorecard) | CEO HR director, HR business partner, Contracts and Legal Departments | 2 weeks |
| Award contract | HR director, HR business partner, tender board (contracts and legal) | |

### E. Conclusions

Total time to contract award will be 17/18 weeks.

The focus above has been on the issues associated with the risks and advantages of contracting out the specified activities. It has not addressed the change management and legal processes which must engage the Stokeshire Council staff that will be affected by this change in working.

# Specimen answers

## PDS People Resourcing examination – November 2003: Section B

### Question 1

The agency has a dual role and contradictions in its business process depending whether you view their objectives from their business client's perspective or the perspective of those who are potential recruits. On the one hand it has to attract people on behalf of the client – so the objective is to find good-quality people. Having then attracted individuals, it must then demonstrate that it can place them with a client business (and so the pressure is to convince the client that it has sourced a competent individual) to continue to attract further people, who it can, at some future time, place with one of its clients. The recruitment agency's revenue source is based upon finding and then placing people into jobs with a client. The more people it can place, the greater the revenue.

We need to improve the success criteria and the fiscal model against which our agency is paid. The relationship we have with our (sole) recruitment agency is historical and was never developed in a logical and systematic manner. It is, therefore, time to formally tender a contract for recruitment services. Recognising that the agency has to make a profit (but not to our detriment), I propose that:

1. We open the process to tender. The current agency is included in the final bid list.

2. The agency is invited to meet to discuss the contract (before negotiation/tender) so that it can understand our business better.

3. A contract is developed based upon a performance management system with:

    - clearly defined success criteria which include some measure of quality and fit (in the organisation) of the newly recruited staff, over and above the usual 'bums on seats' approach – we can invite comments from agencies

    - incentivised payments (based upon the above).

4.  There is a need to build personal and professional relationships based upon a series of regular meetings with fixed agendas that review progress and quality.

5.  We nominate a contract manager from one of our internal business partners to manage the relationship and to act as a focal point for quality and process issues.

## Question 2

For a detailed explanation of the role of interim managers, refer to the CIPD's own *How to* guide on the subject.

What interim managers are about:

*   They are employed on a short-term basis (at middle to senior manager level) to deliver a specific project or to cover a position while a permanent manager is located.

*   They have well-developed managerial skills.

These people are not managers who cannot find long-term permanent roles and are 'temping' until they can. They have chosen the role for whatever reason. Employing 'interims' can have distinct advantages. They can, for example, if employed to change manage an activity, bring to the business a range of specialist skills and also a vision/perspective not influenced or encumbered by the past. Because they have no investment in the future, their decision-making is less likely to be influenced by personal factors (gain of position, power and so on).

Identifying the 'right' person is obviously key so the role and person specification needs careful thought.

On the negative side, interim managers do not have any background in the (our) business and may rush the job because they see fresh contract opportunities appearing on the horizon.

## Question 3

Although age discrimination will not become illegal until 2006 when the United Kingdom adopts the European Union's directive on age discrimination, there are sound business reasons that we should not discriminate on age grounds.

The National Office of Statistics (reiterated in the 1998 and 2004 *Workplace and employment relations survey* by Culley *et al*) indicates that the United Kingdom (and most of Western Europe) is under-going significant demographic changes. Fewer babies are being born (birth rates are falling below the 2.1 children per family needed to maintain a stable population) and adults are living longer. These changes will create a number of business and social issues.

If rolls are falling in our schools, this will eventually impact upon the size of the human resource pool from which we fish for our talent. One option is to recruit older people into our ranks and also to retain those who we would normally see retire from the company at 60 or 65 years of age. B&Q have a policy of recruiting from the older generation (harnessing their lifetime skills) and Barclays have reviewed their policies.

How do we attract and retain our older staff? What are their moti-vations to work? We will have to review and align our HR policies, in terms of:

- flexibility (starting, finishing, part-time and duration of work)

- pensions

- release decisions if there is no 'normal retirement date'.

The UK government is reviewing the impact of the ageing popula-tion and falling demographic roles and, for example, its impact upon pension provisions.

[*Author note*: The article referred to in the question was written by Karen Higginbottom, *People Management*, 5 December 2002. Candi-dates, not unreasonably, may not be able to quote verbatim the key points found in this specific article but they should be aware of the change in demographic trend. It is a 'hot topic' and has been widely reported in the quality press and on television. Future demographic trends may/will have significant impact on their business. We need to reflect upon the specific issues raised by and resourcing problems created by an ageing population and what this means to a tight employment market. Candidates should be aware of the related issue of recruiting within the EU and from non-EU countries to fill vacancies, and the problems this type of activity engenders. Already we are seeing the NHS recruiting nurses from India and the Philip-pines, and haulage firms focusing on the new (post May 2004) EU member states for suitably qualified HGV drivers.]

## Question 4    talent

There have been a number of articles in the press such as the *Sunday Times* (30 August 2003) as well as the article by Susan Annunzio in *People Resourcing* (October 2001), entitled 'How to find and retain talent', where she explores the appropriate processes for retaining, developing and motivating a company's talent. Arguably, according to Jack Welsh (former CEO of GE), management should be occupied with identifying and developing the company's future stock of management. His view is that up to 40 per cent of management time should be dedicated to this task.

Coming back to Annunzio's article, she suggests:

- that the top 20 per cent of the company's ablest staff are identified – those who have potential, those who make the decisions and challenge the norms to improve the organisation

- removing barriers to organisational culture that stifle experimentation – by this she means that, for example the appraisal process should not, on the one hand, encourage experimentation and on the other reproach and punish failure

- ensuring that the remuneration system (pay and benefits) is aligned with the company strategy for talent management

- that the company has a culture of rewarding and praising those who succeed and are making a difference.

In essence the company should have a Performance Management System in place which links the individual people management process elements, in a holistic manner, to support as one of the themes the strategic focus on 'talent management and development'.

There is of course a potential down side to this activity. Those who are not perceived as 'the chosen few' can become disillusioned and thus disconnect from the organisation. Those who engage with the mundane and transactional work are important to the operation, but perhaps do not have the ability to create new wealth, to innovate. Therefore, as with all management process, there has to be a transparency of operation because without this transparency the system is open to corruption, favouritism and nepotism, which defeat the original objective.

## Question 5

[*Author's comment*: Before engaging in answering this question, candidates should reflect on the topic the chief examiner is alluding to. In this situation it is about encouraging 'discretionary behaviour' and strengthening the psychological contract. The theories date back to Maslow and Herzberg. Herzberg, in particular, demonstrated in a famous article (which has since been reprinted in the *Harvard Business Review* of December 2003 but was originally published in 1968) that certain factors which he labelled as 'hygiene factors' (adequate salary and so on), although an important part of the employment relationship and needing to be present, were not the motivators. According to his studies the motivators were extrinsic, and constituted such things as praise and recognition by management. Further studies have shown that having greater autonomy improves satisfaction, which in turn strengthens the bond, the 'psychological contract', between employee and employer. In recent times and important for HR practitioners and CIPD students, this work has been added to by John Purcell *et al* of the University of Bath in the CIPD Research Report (2003) *Understanding the people and performance link: unlocking the black box*. This report is a must for all CIPD professionals, whether or not they are studying towards a qualification. It establishes the link between performance and motivation. Purcell *et al* use terms like 'organisational citizenship' and 'discretionary behaviour' to define how good people mangement is rewarded by staff 'going that extra mile'.

In the chief examiners' report on this question, Ted Johns suggests that candidates could use material from the article by Katie Peters (former head of group HR at Sommerfield) that appeared in *People Management* (October 2002). Peters argues that the company can compensate for its relatively poor (labour) market position by focusing on the quality of its store managers. She states that salary is *in*frequently quoted as a reason why people leave their stores; rather it is the way they are treated, whether the work is challenging and is fun. In essence the store managers bring all these elements together in the microcosm of society which is the store.

There are though other ways to answer this question. The approach I take was suggested by a student (of this author) who 'sat' this paper as a mock examination. She answered in the following way:

Recent research about how to optimise people's performance and commitment can be found in the (2004) *Times* 'Top 100 companies to work for survey', which is an excellent article for understanding the key factors which contribute to motivating people at work. The survey focused on a number of areas:

- leadership: what employees feel about management

- well-being: work/life balance, flexible working, opportunities

- my manager

- giving back to community: corporate social responsibility

- my company: feelings about the company people work for as opposed to those they work with

- the team: the relationship the employee has with his/her colleagues

- fair deal: pay and reward; is my pay in line internally and externally?

- personal growth: am I stretched and challenged, does the company give me opportunity to develop (in line with business objectives)?

The bullet points listed above are in order of merit and so it can be seen that pay and benefits do not sit at the top of the list. We would all like to be paid in the top quartile for our business sector but pragmatically (there is a recognition) that this is not possible. There is sufficient evidence that leads to the conclusion that how we are treated is vital to our satisfaction in the workplace.

## Question 6

It is a complex issue to draw a link between corporate ethicality and people resourcing. The link is essentially in the concept of the talent magnet. There are a number of different factors which when brought together coalesce to identify the company brand; something that people, whether customers, employees or potential employees, can readily identify with. It is linked to reputation management and thus in general terms how the business is perceived to be managed by those outside (the business). It takes time to build but on the other hand, can be quickly destroyed, and so has to be carefully nurtured, and those involved in the (management) process have to demonstrate (in Peter Drucker's terms – they 'walk the talk') that they have embodied the ethical notions that the business espouses.

Businesses that readily come to mind who are recognised to own and espouse particular moral and ethical stands are the Co-Op (branding of its goods) and Body Shop (stance on animal testing). The *Times* Top 100 companies (2004) lists 'best for giving something back' as one of the criteria against which companies are measured. In our postmodern society there is recognition that pay and benefits are but one element in the complex mix that attracts people into work.

## Question 7

[*Author's comment*: on a first reading of this question one could interpret it as asking how *poor quality* employees can be weeded out in the recruitment and selection process. This though is not the intention of the question. The question is about identifying those who seek to gain employment for their own personal ends such as anarchists or paedophiles, that is, those with some criminal intent. It is in essence about the due diligence that resourcing professionals must exercise so that individuals with unlawful intent are barred entry into the organisation.]

Checking and confirming the credentials of prospective employee is a transactional and processual, but nevertheless, vitally important task.

The level of check by business organisations on applicants depends upon the business sector. For example for those who will be working in the education or caring sector, or where they are likely to come into contact with vulnerable individuals, the CRB (Criminal Records Bureau) has to give clearance. For UK nationals, checks can readily be made on references and also on the authenticity of claimed qualifications, either directly with the colleges or through agencies that offer this type of service. When employing guest workers, those without EU citizenship, checks should be made to establish both their identity and their right to work in the United Kingdom, that is, whether have they the appropriate documentation in place. HR professionals should be aware of the need to cross-reference passports with immigration papers and other documentation such as driving licences and identity cards to properly establish the credentials of those applying for work. Rules change, especially with respect to immigrant workers' rights to work, and rights to remain in the United Kingdom, so there is need to have a mechanism that causes the currency of the process to be reviewed.

## Question 8

[*Author's note*: this is a 'bread and butter' question and is testing your basic employment law knowledge. It is about adding value by understanding and applying the fundamentals of employment legislation that governs and underpins the PR process. The question could as easily have been asked about the management of the interview process and the issues of interviewer bias. This is where you have to know your 'stuff' – there are no shortcuts. This model answer is replying to the question posed 'in role'.]

Recent legislative decisions have resulted in a more cautious approach from people giving references. The company stance is that all references should emanate from the HR function – because of the need for consistency. For your information – all data given in a reference should be based on fact or be capable of independent verification. As a guide, references should be fair, accurate and not give a misleading overall impression of the employee. We do not give any subjective opinion about an individual's performance, conduct or suitability, that we cannot substantiate with factual evidence, no matter how much we feel we should help individuals with their job search.

The referee may have a legal liability to the prospective employer. If the referee gives a reference that falsely attributes qualities, or lists other 'material factors' that are known to be untrue, an action alleging deceit could arise. There are a number of pitfalls and legal requirements that cause us to be sensitive over this issue. The legislation (part) that governs references:

- Under The Rehabilitation of Offenders Act 1974 (ROA) an applicant is not obliged to give information regarding any previous convictions ('spent' or otherwise). A number of professions are excluded from ROA, including the medical, legal and accounting professions.

The CIPD produces a Quick facts leaflet on 'Employing people with criminal records' that I can copy and send over to you.

- It should however be noted that the Financial Services and Markets Act 2000 Act applies to the provision of references. Employers engaged in the provision of financial services, as governed by this Act, are bound to supply references.

- The Data Protection Act 1998 will also apply to the processing and storing of information in the provision of a reference.

[*Further author comment*: Stephen Taylor in *People resourcing* acknowledges that there is a paradox which is driven by the competing and changing demands of the current and prospective employer. From the prospective employer's viewpoint the requirement is to obtain as much information as possible, while the perspective of the current employer is to release as little information as possible, because of possible legal implications; yet under the banner of 'duty of care' demonstrate that it is not impeding the opportunity for their employee to better him/herself.]

## Question 9

[*Author's comment*: this is a very specific question and very pertinent to HR professionals who work in multinationals or companies that have internationally seconded staff. The research is very specific about the qualities an individual should posses to give him or her a chance of making a success of an assignment.

A good pass would be obtained by:

- detailing and explaining the factors that should be assessed when appointing a person for an international role

- quoting the relevant literature

- discussing the need to involve the family in the process (for accompanied postings).]

The impact of failing to employ appropriate criteria to the selection of staff for international assignments is severe and costly. It is costly for the company, in both time and money – time lost having to re-recruit, recruitment costs and the loss of business while the recruitment process is repeated a second time. This does not consider the 'cost' in both financial and social terms for the individual.

Research shows, and there are a number of typologies that have been brought together in the CIPD research report called *HR and globalisation* (Harris, Brewster and Sparrow 2001), that there is a requirement to assess a range of attributes and competencies:
*Personal characteristics*

- flexibility

- a desire to adjust

- cultural empathy

- tolerance of ambiguity

- leadership qualities

- self-confidence

- emotional stability.

*Language ability*
*Previous international experience* – there is a strong correlation between previous overseas experience and future successes.
*Accompanying partner:* Black *et al* (1999) found that many international assignments fail because accompanying spouses/partners are unable to settle (they quote a number of reasons). The implication from their work is that the spouse should be included in the selection – or perhaps the de-selection process.

## Question 10

Competency frameworks are generally backward looking and so have a 'shelf life'. It can be, in this quickly moving technological age, a time-consuming occupation to maintain the currency and relevance of competency frameworks to any given role. One can also imagine that the competencies required to work in self-managed teams are very specific (behaviours, attitudes, interpersonal skills) and are of key importance to ensure a fit of the new candidate into the existing team. Common sense suggests that team members should be involved in the preparation of an appropriate framework, thus engendering ownership. Returning to the question posed: the competency framework can be made more relevant by:

- focusing on few core competencies that apply to all staff

- only including key role and a limited number of functional competencies

- describing individual competencies in specific behavioural terms.

The above has to be predicated on an understanding by all as to what each competence means in real terms. This implies that there is a need for training or facilitation of discussion groups of those who will be involved in the selection process.

# Sample paper:
# PDS People Resourcing examination – May 2003

## Section A: case study

*It is permissible to make assumptions by adding to the case study details given below provided the essence of the case study is neither changed nor undermined in any way by what is added.*

Industrial Mecanica de Salvador S.A. (IMS) is a family company situated in Salvador, Brazil, manufacturing circular valves mainly for the country's oil industry. Some years ago the company's chief executive officer (CEO) decided to make some changes in his company's traditional paternalistic, command-and-control structure in order to introduce a more participative management approach. A quarterly profit distribution plan was introduced, whereby 7.5 per cent of net profits would be paid to employees in proportion to their salary levels, and another 7.5 per cent distributed evenly to all employees. Thus even the lowest paid staff received a significant share of the company's profits.

The results were electrifying. Within weeks of the first profit distribution, a cost-reduction programme and an in-house training scheme – aimed at improving the skill base of the employees and upgrade the quality of the firm's products – had been introduced by the workforce themselves. Antagonistic personnel attitudes and poor working conditions gave way to a climate of co-operation and improvements in the employees' cultural, emotional and spiritual lives.

At a recent quarterly meeting, two machinists complained that their supervisors took too long to respond to requests for help. A 30-minute debate ensued, after which the employees' assembly proposed to eliminate the role of supervisor, replacing it with the job of 'consultant'.

Although hesitant at first, the employees now feel free to call upon the best 'consultants' whenever they have a problem. The 'consultants', in turn, have an incentive to provide quality service to their 'clients' because, if they don't, they have no right to be in the factory.

The general feeling at IMS is that quality of life, including life in the workplace, is reflected in the quality of the product. It is also accepted, moreover, that a right to a share is accompanied by a share in responsibility in the case of any losses. At IMS, workers help absorb the company's losses, when they occur, by deferring overtime payments and occasionally accepting short-run wage/salary reductions. Clearly, however, none of this can happen without frank and open information sharing – transparency – which helps everyone's understanding of the company's performance, its activities, its future strategies, costs and profits.

You are the Human Resources (HR) manager in a similarly sized yet hierarchical conventional UK-based manufacturing company, which is currently in difficulties. Your CEO, Dr Tomkinson, has read about the experience of IMS and has even visited the company's plant in order to see for himself. Believing the IMS model to be your own firm's ultimate salvation, he is determined to introduce an IMS-type culture in his own company.

With this in mind, Dr Tomkinson has asked you to present proposals to address the PR implications. At the same time, he recognises that it may not be entirely straightforward to transfer all aspects of the IMS experience into your own firm, and because of his own research background he needs to be reassured that there is convincing evidence to support any claims you make.

Produce a report for your CEO, which addresses the following issues:

1. The lessons (from both research and organisational experience) about the problems associated with a shift of people resourcing philosophies, procedures and practices from those currently found in your own company to those which characterise IMS, plus some evidence-based proposals about how to make the changes easier to accomplish and assimilate.

2. The methods of implementing the new philosophy with specific regard to replacing existing supervisors by 'consultants', namely:

- the proposed competency framework for the consultant role
- the selection methods to be used
- the actions to be taken in the case of existing supervisors who do not wish to become 'consultants' or who lack the necessary attributes.

In all cases, you should give reasons for your proposals, and your recommendations should be reinforced with references to relevant research material and benchmarking evidence from other organisations that may have undergone similar transitions.

[*Your report should give approximately equal attention to each of the above two issues.*]

## Section B

Answer SEVEN of the ten questions in this section. To communicate your answers more clearly you may use whatever methods you wish, for example diagrams, flow charts, bullet points, so long as you provide an explanation of each.

You should assume that having arrived at your place of work, you have just switched on your PC and the following 10 e-mails appear on your screen. You are required to indicate the content of your proposed response; the method through which you transmit your response (by e-mail, face-to-face discussion, etc.) need not be specified.

1. *From a friend employed in the Human Resources (HR) function for another organisation*: We're thinking about the introduction of a performance review system with rating scales. I am uneasy, however. What does research say about the problems with rating scales and about how such problems can be overcome?
2. *From your mentor*: I know that you're preparing for your CIPD exams, so here's a question for you. Anderson and Shackleton (1993) list many reasons why selection interviews have been attacked for their poor predictive validity.

What do you think are the main ones? Explain why the selection interview continues to be so popular in your own organisation.

3. *From your HR Director*: Managers frequently tell me that someone working for them is 'good' at their job, and when I ask them what they mean they can't tell me. How do you define 'good' in this context?

4. *From the Sales and Service Director*: We're shortly going to search for people to work in our new call centre, and we think we should be looking for extroverts. However, I thought I should check with you before we start. Do you think we are on the right lines, or do you have any better advice – preferably delivered from authoritative research evidence?

5. *From the Finance Director*: Your function has already over-spent on its recruitment-advertising budget, so it's time to consider new approaches. I have a feeling that e-recruitment could be more cost-effective – what do you think?

6. *From a Business Unit Manager (retail outlet)*: As you know, we don't have our own HR team, so I am dependent on you for keeping me up to date. I understand last month (April 2003) some new employment rights came into effect. Can you summarise and explain the main ones for me, please?

7. *From a journalist working for* People Management: We're planning a feature about women in organisations, and our start point is the claim by Herminia Ibarra (*Financial Times*, 7 December 2001) that 'No world-class company has solved the problem of retaining and promoting women.' Even where women are hired at equal entry levels in equal proportion to men, that 50 per cent dwindles to less than 10 per cent at senior levels. What practical steps could an organisation take to address this situation?

8. *From the IT Manager*: Something caught my eye the other day – I was reading an article about the learning organisa-tion. The authors claim that the secret lies in the 'mix' between practices and people. What did they mean?

9. *From the Chief Executive Officer*: What's all this I keep hearing about a 'war for talent'? What's the evidence?

10. *From the HR Director*: In October last year, the government launched a consultation paper on widening the scope of the

Working Time Directive, and I read in *People Management* that some commentators are calling for a statutory 35-hour week. OK, this may not happen, but can you please outline the implications for people resourcing if it did?

**END OF EXAMINATION**

# Specimen answers

## PDS People Resourcing examination – May 2003: Section A

### QA 1

**Strictly confidential – draft proposal**

**Tomkinson Quality Machine Components**

A Vision for the Future – a turnaround strategy

A report compiled by A. G. Candidate

**Contents of Section A**

Examiners, please note:
QA part 1 is answered primarily in Section A and Section B, B1 of the report
QA part 2 is answered primarily in Section B2 through to B5 of the report

## Section A: Background summary

Changing the culture of a company is probably one of the most difficult tasks to achieve. There are a number of models that can be called upon to help bring about the desired change. Barbara Senior in her book *Organisational change* and Charles Handy, who has written a series of texts about organisational change, have greatly added to the general understanding of the change process.

Classically, we have to understand where we are in terms of our People Resourcing environment and consider where we would like to be. We can then understand the differences between the future (desired state) and the present, and so better bring about the change.

Our company can be characterised as hierarchical, with differentials between management, technical and manual labouring staff. The company is unionised and with a generally good employee relationship. The unions mainly become involved during the annual pay negotiations or whenever, for example, there is a grievance or disciplinary action.

We have operated in the same location for the past 30 years and are generally perceived locally as a 'good' employer. Recruitment tends to be from the local labour market, traditionally the sons and daughters of our existing employees. We are known as a family business. This has its advantages and disadvantages. To improve our competitive position, you have indicated that we need to introduce new technology; concomitant with the technological change generally experienced throughout industry and we also need to attract some better-qualified talent, especially technicians and engineers. This means that our recruitment net needs to be expanded. As you know, we have seen new competition come into the market from overseas and slowly chip away at our customer base.

There is a need to do things differently but whatever we do has to 'fit' into the organisational paradigm on which we would like to build.

## Section B: Vision for the future

What type of organisation would we like to build that will take us forward for the next ten to 15 years? Consider the accompanying table, which has been quickly put together. The management team can add further meat on the bone but the drift is clear.

**Table 1** Today and tomorrow

| Current situation | Future vision |
|---|---|
| Management processes closed and secretive | These processes will truly have to be open and managers will have to 'walk the talk' |
| Direction from supervisor (management-led) | *Overall* – direction from management but intermediate goals by self-motivated teams |
| Supervisors decides when/ how work is accomplished, task-specific | Teams and individuals become empowered to make these decisions |
| Promotion to supervisory/ management initially through technical competence | Supervisors become facilitators/ consultants |
| We are very hierarchical | We will probably have to restructure with a flatter organisation (groan – we have heard it all before!) – so that the organisation reflects the way we wish to communicate |
| Recruitment focused on technical competence | Technical competence is a starting point, basis to be considered by us – key recruitment decisions need to based on fit, largely associated with interpersonal skills |
| Training and development – largely management-directed | Individuals and teams need significantly greater say in their development |
| Performance management – annual appraisal, largely management-led, focus on delivery of hard targets | More involvement of staff in the process (design also?). Need to recognise and to focus on softer issues of people leadership, good teamworker and of course rewarding teams, rather than individuals |

The table is incomplete: for example, nothing has been said about remuneration practices that could/should be adopted.

There has been a recent article in *People Management* (one of the January 1998 editions), entitled 'Profitable Personal', by Michael West of Sheffield Hallam University. It details what happened when a UK company embarked upon a programme of improved employee involvement in the workplace and the resulting positive outcomes. This would be a good starting point to consider what practices we could usefully employ to bring about the change we desire.

## Section C: Implications for the future

### 1 Communication and change plan

To make the changes possible we will have to communicate effectively, at all levels, and to involve all our staff in the process. Consider the following draft communication plan (after Kurt Lewin): management and supervisory staff will have to be 'brought on board' at an early stage, once the management team have agreed the direction that we need to take. All management and supervisors will have to be trained in how we wish them to communicate with their people and so start to live the message. Once we have the management on board then we would need to bring in the unions and explain to them the situation we face, our plans and strategy.

#### *1.1 Draft process for change*

- Explain the current situation and engender an understanding why we cannot continue in the way we do business.

- Deliver our vision for the future and elicit feedback. We need to take notice of this feedback by using the suggestions from staff focus groups. Perhaps we should put together a change team from different parts of the business (start as we mean to go on) facilitated by a quality consultant (from outside).

- Take note of employee feedback and develop a plan of action with various groups in the organisation.

- Start to bring about that change by restructuring/delayering – whatever we decide.

- Start to train staff how to work in teams, to help them understand what is expected of them and at the same time move to finalising the design of the business.

- By this time, it will be necessary to roll out some of the interim outputs of the change and elicit more feedback – communication needs to be regular and informative (pragmatic).

- Complete the change process and start to work on any of the issues that have arisen.

- Finally – test the 'temperature' to see how (if) things are beginning to embed.

2 Roles and responsibilities (QA2)

Above all, you, as CEO, will have to champion the change. Total commitment from your management and supervisory team is vital for this major change event to stand any chance of working. A culture change is very difficult, but not impossible to bring about.

In some respects our supervisory, especially first-line management staff, are going to be the most affected by these stages. They will probably feel that they are losing status, self-respect, and will have perhaps myriad other feelings. Some, of course, will be aware that other firms in this sector have been successful in going part way in the direction that we intend to go and have embraced the changes. Others will not be so keen and will feel threatened. We must make and take time to explain these changes to all our people. Not all will be able to make the transition from supervisor to internal consultant.

The move to becoming an *internal consultant* does *not* mean that the individual is a 'yes' man or woman but someone whom I would expect to be able to make value judgements on informed opinion and make recommendations on logic, not on what people want to hear. This has implications for our management staff. Some of our senior managers are also going to have to address their interpersonal skills and, for example, not take personal issue on a challenge to a decision or proposal they may have made. People will have to think differently and work more co-operatively as part of a team.

3 New competencies

Can I suggest the following list of knowledge skills and attributes (KSAs), which we would expect our consultants to exhibit? Technical competence – in whatever area they working in – opens the door to becoming an internal consultant but does not guarantee entry. However, they will all be required to have or to eventually develop mastery of the following competencies:

- Good interpersonal skills, empathy, understanding.

- Personal confidence/strength of character.

- Resilience to fight one's corner.

- Good negotiation skills.

The above is an incomplete draft. We should involve our staff in helping to decide what sort of framework would best suit our desired culture.

Too few of our people really understand our business or the environment within which it operates. So, added to the above we could seek to develop a broader understanding of the business in all our managers and consultants (by increasing learning, job rotation and so on).

4  Recruitment and Selection in Tomkinson Quality Machine Parts
This could perhaps be better achieved by using assessment centres with some situational exercises etc. as the selection vehicle. We already have *some* people who probably fit into the type of consultant role that we envisage, and together with our change consultant, we could put some meat on the assessment programme.

For new staff we would have to consider seriously how to recruit and select, but again probably use the assessment centre approach. The consultant role will be instrumental in the facilitation of teams. We could manage a blend of internal development of our existing staff, who meet the profile, plus graduate/professional recruitment. Note: Assessment centres (Smith, quoted in Taylor, S. (2002), *People resourcing*) are one of the better predictors but expensive. However, for this type of role it is so critical it will be worth the expense.

5  Practical and legal considerations
This is a 'nutty one' to answer but our circumstances are such that we cannot shrink away from our responsibilities. The options are:

- Limited opportunities for redeployment – with retraining in other roles.

- Some of our staff could be offered early retirement.

- Redundancy with outplacement support.

From a legal standpoint, we should consider that there could be some redundancies from this change 'exercise'. We would have to declare an at-risk situation in accordance with the employment law. The unions by this time will have been brought on board so the process will be purely a formal recognition of the facts, but we would have to work with all involved parties.

I would consider that staff would have to apply for their jobs under the new organisation. We could ring-fence certain areas, so focusing on those staff at risk.

I will be happy to discuss issues further.

# Specimen answers

## PDS People Resourcing examination – May 2003: Section B

### Question 1

In essence, many, but not all, of the problems are associated with the person performing the appraisal. Appraisers tend to focus their ratings around the mid-point of the scale (*skewed central tendency*) and not use either the excellents or the poor/weak indicators, those points at the ends of the scale. Scales are too woolly, with terms like good, average etc., there being insufficient definition around the scale points. Some appraisers also consider how they (thought) they did the job and mark current incumbents down.

How can it be improved? By training, holding workshops to achieve a mutual understanding of the issues and measurements involved, so bringing about a more unified standard. Some companies, especially large mature operations, bring in a forcing function, which restricts the grading so that, for example 10 per cent of staff are rated as excellent, 30 per cent are very good and the remainder are satisfactory, with some poor performers. The rankings, before being finalised, are reviewed by a peer management group where at least two managers/supervisors must know the person being assessed.

[*Author's comment:* In this question candidates were expected to answer both parts of the question; what are the issues; how can they be solved (or at least ameliorated)?]

### Question 2

Stephen Taylor (2002), *People resourcing,* lists the major reasons why interviews have been attacked for their poor predictive validity. In his work, he quotes Smith et al. The major reasons have been listed below:

- The similar-to-me effect – looking for someone in one's own image.

- The self-fulfilling prophecy effect – where the interviewer has asked questions that will naturally lead to a desired conclusion.

- The prototyping effect – the interviewer has gone into the interview with a pre-programmed expectation of the type of person he/she would like to see in the job.

- The halo-and-horns effect – the interview is affected by personal appearance.

- The expectancy effect – where the CV has unduly influenced the interviewer's perception of the candidate.

- The personal liking effect – no comment.

Interviews remain popular although their validity (below 0.3) is poor because, for those conducting them, there is a high degree of face validity; managers like to be involved with the recruitment of staff who will work in their department; moreover, many interviewers fallaciously consider that they are excellent interviewers.

[*Author's comment:* Candidates are not asked how they can improve the interview process, but one can imagine that this could form the basis of a similar question in future papers. Stick to what has been asked because time is of essence. Some, not all, of the bullet pointed responses, have attracted comment to explain their meaning. Those that are sufficiently self-explanatory have been left with no comment. This is an individual's 'call' when answering the question.

The candidate has not systematically answered with all the possible options as described in the core text (Taylor 2002, pp173–174) because the answers provided here are an attempt to reflect what is expected in an examination given the restrictions of time.]

## Question 3

What does 'good' mean in the context of work? Does it mean competent or perhaps effective in terms of delivering goals and objectives (CIPD studies by Guest and Purcell)? This can be related back to the CIPD's concept of a 'thinking performer'. Explicit in this is having an understanding of the essential knowledge for the role, the skills to be able to deliver and the ability to reflect upon the options and decide upon a course of action, and so apply the knowledge and bring about a desired outcome.

Added to the above is the notion of going beyond contract or the constraints of the job description, what has elsewhere been termed as OCB (organisational citizenship behaviour), to deliver and to meet customer requirements and accepting personal responsibility for outcomes.

Perhaps we should be thinking of process definitions rather than a definition that focuses simply on results, because the route to achieving an end often is as equally as important as the result.

[*Author's comment*: Of course, some may define 'good' in other ways, for example, purely in terms of the individual's compatibility with his/her peers and group/team members. In general, however, a definition of the adjective 'good' in this context is likely to provoke some discussion of the 'Thinking Performer' concept as above.]

## Question 4

The evidence suggests that extroverts are *not* appropriate for call-centre work: they talk too much, they are poor listeners, they become bored quickly, and then they either leave or start behaving mischievously.

So what type of person is best suited to this role? It would be preferable to seek mild introverts with a low superego in the work situation (so that they can put up with constant rebuffs, if that happens to be the nature of the call-centre activity), a high level of interpersonal skills and certainly a measure of what Britannic Assurance calls 'altruism', i.e. the willingness to think of situations from the perspective of the other person. Do not let age be a factor here because the more mature people are likely to be more settled and not have unrealistic expectations of the role/interaction with the public.

[*Author's comment*: This is one of those questions where you either know the required response or you do not know it – there is no half way. This type of question makes the choice easy – to include or exclude from your list to questions to answer during your initial assessment of Section B.]

## Question 5

Initial investigations suggest that e-recruitment might *not* be the panacea for which we are all looking. There are a number of relevant factors to be taken into account: e-recruitment only works efficiently when the organisation has a significant number of posts to fill, across a large geographical area, e.g. graduate trainees, sales representatives, the military, and so forth. Because e-recruitment encourages applications from manifestly unsuitable candidates, some form of electronic screening must be deployed.

For e-recruitment to work, moreover, potential applicants need (a) internet access and (b) awareness of our e-recruitment initiative. Neither of these can be taken for granted, unless the company is an employer 'brand', e.g. Cadbury Schweppes, Asda and the like. We are not in that league, so for us we would probably need to source any internet recruitment to a specialist agency, so again this militates against sole use of this type of vehicle for recruitment. Now we advertise in specialist journals for our professional staff. These organisations tend to have their own electronic jobs board, as do the newspapers in which we advertise.

So, to sum up, I don't think that we can go it alone with simply having our own internet site – we wouldn't be able to attract the people we need, but we need to invest in our own system because this is the way business is moving. We will still have to rely upon agencies, and press advertising, for the foreseeable future.

[*Author's comment*: Candidates should be aware of the advantages and disadvantages of all forms of recruitment and selection processes.]

## Question 6

Many of these new rights are concerned with the employee's ability to seek the opportunity to work flexibly, especially for working parents with children under the age of six and those who have children with disability under the age of 16.

If a request is made, the organisation must respond within 14 days and only has a limited number of grounds on which a request for flexible working may be refused.

It is associated with the government's response to encourage firms to develop family friendly policies. We are reasonably ahead of the game, so to speak, in this respect because of our *Work/Life Balance* initiative, which is in line with current government thinking – the DTI (Department of Trade and Industry) website gives more details.

[*Author's comment:* Again this is one of those questions where you either know the required response or you don't, so could be easy to include or exclude from your list to questions to answer during your initial assessment of which Section B questions to answer.]

## Question 7

Response to *People Management* journalist:
The 1998 WERS survey (Cully et al. (2002), *Britain at Work as depicted by the 1998 Workplace Employee Relations Survey*) confirms that women are still under-represented in senior managerial positions. The fact that they constitute circa 50 per cent of all employment positions is due in the main to their significant representation in part-time employment, clerical, service type work. This issue is part of the management of the larger issue of the management of diversity.

Research shows that more women voluntarily leave employment earlier than their male counterparts due to concerns about balancing work and family life. Couple this with the social 'work issue' that women have yet still to break through the glass ceiling – one only needs to read the recent high-profile tribunal cases involving discriminatory practices against women– then there is no wonder why female representation reduces by the time female cohorts are ready to move into senior management positions.

A number of options are open, specifically:

- Improve legal, family policy ..... flexible working and home working for periods of time, career break ..... and job share. Government legislation gives some way to move employers in this direction.

- Change cultures, which positively encourage diversity (Shell intends to have 20 per cent of its senior executive positions filled by females at the end of 2004 ..... *People Management*). Many large businesses have appointed ..... iversity Directors' to raise the level of the issue and at the same time give a clear positive message. Ford Motors, for example.

This, in reality, is not just a moral issue ..... but also an economic necessity. Once you've appreciated it may be too late!

[Author's comment: This type of issue will not go away and candidates are advised to watch the *People Management* journal for relative articles on diversity, labour market trends (and the reasons – demographics, etc.) and the options open to business, together with examples of initiatives taken. Candidates should also be aware of the WERS survey (see References), which is conducted every four years, the last published version being about the outcomes of the 1998 census of UK industry.]

## Question 8

The issue raised (re the learning organisation) relates to what is currently understood to be knowledge management and intellectual and social capital theory (John Storey has written at length about this topic).

In essence, it is not simply good enough to employ intelligent and individually motivated people (intellectual capital), but we must bring about a sharing of knowledge by processes that encourage this activity.

We can recruit people in the type of image (knowledge, skills and attributes), which, we as a company, value then we must put the processes in place (knowledge management), which further encourage a sharing of knowledge and thus corporate learning. Even our performance management systems must reflect what we are trying to achieve. It is about the 'fit' of processes so that when 'bundled' or aligned together they all form part of a coherent HR package. Generating piecemeal initiatives will usually cause confusion and produce no meaningful benefits.

[*Author's comment*: Understanding the key issues of what is meant by intellectual capital, social capital, knowledge management and emotional intelligence is important for today's PR professional.]

## Question 9

The evidence for a 'war for talent' is highly ambiguous. It is real in the case of organisations that operate in a highly competitive, highly innovative, knowledge-based environment, where the concept of 'human capital' does make sense, and where competitive advantage is largely attributable to a very small number of 'core competents' (often only one per cent of the total workforce) whose expertise is very rare and who, therefore, could not be easily replaced.

The idea of a 'war for talent' is less relevant for organisations functioning in a relatively stable and even non-competitive environment, since the need for innovation in such enterprises is far less self-evident.

The above description focuses on the types of individual but the issue cannot be divorced from the 'tightness' of the labour market.

The implications for us are that we should be identifying those who have the skills and knowledge and be considering the options (for development, retention, etc.) in terms of HR planning. There was a short article about Capitol One bank's approach to people development and selection for senior posts in *The Times*, 30 March 2003. They positively identify their talent and have a long-term plan in place to develop them.

## Question 10

We, in the UK, have some exemptions to the Working Time Directive; junior doctors are one such group. Staff can opt out of some of the restrictions at present but this might change (Taylor, S. 2002).

If nobody were allowed to work more than a 48-hour week or, even more stringently, a 35-hour week, there would of course be some consequences because we have less time to get the job done given that we would probably not wish to increase staff numbers. (France has introduced this legislation with that in mind – to reduce unemployment.)

In essence, business would:

- probably start taking more interest in people productivity, multiskilling and so forth

- probably show greater reluctance to employ full-time or even part-time people

- instead engage fixed-term contract workers (at a higher level, organisations would be likely to use consultants rather more).

The consequence is that people in the labour market with no identifiable skills would find it much harder to gain employment, and to that extent, it is likely that differential rewards within organisations may become more pronounced.

[*Author's comment*: There are clearly a number of options open to management should legislation be changed. This type of question offers candidates an opportunity to demonstrate their ability to think around the subject and give considered opinion about likely outcomes based upon informed opinion. One needs only to go back to David Guest's model of the HRM environment and Atkinson's model of the flexible firm to obtain a 'directional steer'.]

**END OF EXAMINATION**

# PDS People Resourcing practice examination

The following Section A and Section B questions have either been taken from previous examinations, some set under the PQS scheme, the June 2002 specimen PR examination (marked 'SP'), or have been developed by the author (marked 'AQ'). All are representative in style, content and standard to the level required under the new PDS scheme.

## Section A: case study (November 2002)

*It is permissible to make assumptions by adding to the case study details given below provided the essence of the case study is neither changed nor undermined in any way by what is added.*

Katherine and Peter Lim are two Singapore entrepreneurs who have successfully pioneered the Beautiful Living retail chain across the Asia Pacific region. Modelled originally on Anita Roddick's Body Shop, the Beautiful Living Empire nonetheless has a number of distinctive features, which have given it a competitive advantage of its own. Firstly, the Lims both hold strong ethical views (they are practising Christians), and the openness of their business practices has often been contrasted favourably with the dubious claims made by the Body Shop about, for example, animal testing. Secondly, the Lims have not attempted to emulate the high personal profile pursued by Anita Roddick: instead, they have remained in the background, leaving their franchise holders to act as ambassadors for their values. Thirdly, the Beautiful Living group has diversified its products and services so that it now offers health and fitness programmes, health foods/drinks, stress management therapies, work/life balance counselling and a general framework of lifestyle enhancement activities.

Now it is time for Beautiful Living to enter the European market place, initially by opening 50 retail units in the United Kingdom. The company's worldwide Internet sales have already convinced Katherine and Peter Lim that there is potential in the United Kingdom, and they in turn have persuaded a group of Malaysian investors to provide the investment to enable the project to get off the ground.

Because the success of Beautiful Living so far has been largely attributed to the firm yet unobtrusive leadership offered by the Lims, they intend to play a major part in ensuring that things go right from the start. Each of the 50 retail outlets will be operated by a franchisee, carefully chosen to ensure an appropriate mix of ethicality and business acumen. Each franchisee will be required to supply a personal investment of £100,000 but will be guaranteed a generous share of profits.

Management of the franchise process will be meticulously detailed to ensure total conformity with the Beautiful Living brand image. Staffing is considered to be a key ingredient for the maintenance and projection of this image, but as the vast majority of the franchisees will have no direct experience of recruitment, selection or staff management, and will not have access to professional help (especially in the early stages), it is essential that they are given clear guidance on how to proceed.

Katherine and Peter Lim have commissioned you to produce the 'People Resourcing Guidelines', which will become part of the instructions issued to all Beautiful Living franchisees. Present your draft proposals for these guidelines, under each of the following three chapter titles:

1. how to select the right people for Beautiful Living
2. how to avoid the legal pitfalls associated with recruitment and selection
3. how to get the most out of the people you employ.

[*You should devote approximately equal amounts of time and space to each of the above requirements.*]

## Section B

Answer SEVEN of the ten questions in this section. To communicate your answers more clearly you may use whatever methods you wish, for example diagrams, flow charts, bullet points, so long as you provide an explanation of each.

You should assume that having arrived at your place of work, you have just switched on your PC and the following ten e-mails appear on your screen. You are required to indicate the content of your proposed response; the method through which you transmit your response (by e-mail, face-to-face discussion, etc.) need not be specified.

1. As a senior HR business partner of a consulting firm you were asked for your understanding of the term 'Knowledge Management'. Briefly indicate your response and indicate five ways in which the HR department could support knowledge management within your business.          (AQ)

2. National Health Service Trust hospitals have experienced and still experience difficulties retaining and recruiting sufficient midwives. There has been a steady loss from the service of competent staff who have found it more 'accommodating' to work as agency staff rather than as direct employees of the NHS. Current estimates indicate that there is a shortfall of in excess of 5.7 per cent of midwives across the UK and 6.3 per cent in England (Royal College of Midwives: Evidence for the Review Body, 2002).
   What would you consider are the options for improving the position?
   • In the short to medium term?
   • long term?          (AQ)

3. Working in central London as a HR business partner to a company employing some 500 workers, many of whom are employed in virtual customer relations departments, responding to e-mail, telephone and fax communications, you are constantly beset by recruitment and retention problems.
   You have been asked by one of your line managers to review the options:
   • to reduce staff turnover
   • to tap into alternative reservoirs of talent.
   What would your response be to this request?
   *Similar* to May 2002 (AQ)

4. Some research suggests that good-looking people, those with optimistic and enthusiastic attitudes and a sense of humour, are more likely (a) to get jobs, and (b) to gain career advancement. What are the psychological principles

involved in this phenomenon? What are the dangers for management? (SP)

5. New legislation, which affects the Data Protection Act, comes into force this year, 2003. Prior to a recruitment exercise, as an HR Adviser to the Operations Department of your firm you decide to conduct a short awareness seminar on the key relative aspects of the DPA for line managers who will be involved in the process. Detail the key advice you would give your managers about the activity to ensure that the process is orchestrated in a fair and transparent manner. (AQ)

6. As HR manager of an operating company of a large multi-national organisation you are requested to assist the CIPD in some work it is preparing on the management of expatriate staff. It is interested in your views as to what factors you would identify as the 'six key ingredients' for effective resourcing policies and practices related to the assignment overseas for employees. (SP)

7. *From your CEO*: 'I'm speaking next week at a CIPD seminar on "The future of work". Brief me on four major trends that will affect working patterns in the UK over the next five years.' (SP)

8. 'Appraisals are about continuous performance improvement. If your appraisal system doesn't achieve this, chuck it out,' robustly claims Mary Budd (quoted in *Management Today*, December 2001). Your comments, please so far as the system used in your own organisation. (May 2002)

9. According to the available research evidence, what are the best ways of predicting whether a candidate will perform successfully on the job or not? Give reasons for your views. (May 2002)

10. *From a fellow CIPD student working for a local authority*: Have you read about the government's campaign to improve public services? My council wants to be proactive about this, so how can we ensure that our resourcing practices reflect what the government wants us to do? (SP)

**END OF EXAMINATION**

# Specimen answers

## PDS People Resourcing practice examination – Section A

### Recruitment and selection for Beautiful Living

A draft proposal

A report compiled by A. G. Consultant

### Contents of Section A

Examiners, please note:
QA1 is answered in Sections A, B and C
**QA2 is answered in Section D**
QA3 is answered in Section E

### Section A: Management summary

For each shop or group of shops, there are two distinct roles that have to be resourced:

- shop manager

- sales assistant.

*After discussion with the franchiser and franchisees, agreement has been reached on the selection criteria. These will be based on a number of key competencies, both skill and behavioural (essentially select for attitude and train for skill) coupled with previous relevant experience. Having the relevant experience (to each role) will be the first hurdle that candidates will need to overcome.*

All candidates, whether considered for the management or sales assistant role, will be expected to have a similar ethical outlook in terms of respect for others (cultural considerations), to be open, frank yet sensitive. The objective is to develop teams that are self-starters, so it is important to identify candidates for the management position who would be comfortable working towards a facilitator or coach role. *To assist in the process of recruitment and selection and future HR support an outsourced HR function (e.g. Accenture Services) will be contracted to assist with the initial interview process and, under my direction, coach all involved staff. The HR contract agency will then provide HR support for all shops for a period of two years. A member of the HR team will be present at each location to assist and be present at all interviews.*

Because the franchisees have little experience in the retail business, the strategy will be to recruit staff with previous experience for all roles until competence has been built within the organisation before taking on inexperienced people.

### Section B: The recruitment and selection process

The recruitment and selection process will be by:

- Advertising in the local and regional press. Candidates will be sent a standard application form focused on the needs of the role, an accountability profile and person specification based upon the competency profile developed with the Lims and the franchisers.

- Depending on numbers applying for the roles, first-cut candidates will be telephone-interviewed and those successful will be asked for face-to-face interviews.

- Selection will be by structured interview – note because of the diverse location of the shops and low numbers involved in each location assessment centres are deemed too expensive. A trained franchisee (they want to see who they are recruiting), with myself or someone from the HR support contractors will, as previously stated, be present at each interview.

## 1 Managerial position

Part of the recruitment process was to ask candidates who were applying for the management position to indicate, in no more than a half to one page of A4 of typewritten script, how they would describe their management style and why they think it works. For those candidates who have not managed people before yet have relevant experience they will be asked how they would manage people and what type of problems they might envisage. For both roles candidates are requested to give an example where their tact and diplomatic skills were tested to their limits.

Behavioural
- Good communication and interpersonal skills, sense of humour.

- Self-starter.

- Sense of customer awareness and service.

- Previous managerial experience in similar relevant environment or has potential.

- Tactful, diplomatic and pragmatic (good customer-facing skills).

Knowledge and experience (skills)
- Previous knowledge and experience of retail work.

- Business-focused – understands the balance sheet and the need to deliver on targets.

- Numerate and literate (written and IT).

- Has potential for development.

## 2 Assistant position

Candidates will be asked to write, in no more than a half to one page of A4 of typewritten script, how they approach work – what motivates them in their work and what interest they get out of it, what they can bring to the role and why they are applying to Beautiful Living for a job. Candidates will be requested to give an example where their tact and diplomacy was tested to its limits.

Behavioural

- Good communication and interpersonal skills, sense of humour.
- Self-starter.
- Sense of customer awareness and service.
- Ready to learn and try new things.
- Tactful, diplomatic and pragmatic (good customer-facing skills).
- Has potential for development.

Knowledge and experience (skills)

- Previous knowledge and experience of retail work.
- Business-focused – understands the balance sheet and the need to deliver on targets.
- Numerate and literate (written and IT).
- The skills required of the assistant are not unlike those required of the manager but clearly focused primarily at the customer.

### 3  Selection: general comments

The selection will be planned as follows:

- Psychometric testing – personality profiling; numerical aptitude; reasoning ability.
- Semi-structured interview (review application form + structured questions about hypothetical scenarios and personal experiences – the candidate's written A4 profile will be used as a starting point (did they write it?) for discussion).

Note: the profiling etc will have to be conducted by competent staff – it is expected that the HR agency will provide this facility. Feedback of the results will be provided to candidates.

### Section C: Training of selection team

Franchisees will be involved in the selection process, therefore they will have to be trained in appropriate techniques. This will be done in a number of one- or two-day events around the UK and will address:

- Interview techniques, need for good preparation, pitfalls of interviewing (biasing, halo effect, recruiting in my own image, temporal effects, etc.), open/closed questioning techniques, role play etc

- Legal requirements of recruitment and selection, pitfalls to be aware of.

### Section D: Legal consideration when recruiting and selecting

Prior to the awareness training day all staff involved in the recruitment and selection process will be given copies of the *People Management*, 'How to ...' guides and ACAS guides on Recruitment and Selection. Training will be given on issues relating to:

- Questions associated with sexist and racist views

- Disability discrimination – access to interview facilities

- Implications of the Data Protection Act – availability of interview notes should candidates request to see them.

*A HR specialist will be present at each interview to:*

- provide a check and balance during the interview and sounding board after the event

- ensure legal compliance during the conduct of the interview.

### Section E – How to get the most out of our of people

This is about motivation and how, therefore, people are managed and treated. It is about:

- Involvement techniques
    - Communication – the Lims are very open, and so developing a communication system that is two-way and therefore involves staff in the business will be in line with the company mould
    - Creating a culture that values people and their views.

- Performance management
    - which recognises the worth and developability of individuals to contribute

-     – which monitors and rewards progress in delivering objectives
-     – which encourages staff to assimilate the behavioural characteristics of the firm.

- Encouraging teamwork and managers to become facilitators.

- Having a reward system that is part of the overall strategy of managing people and reflects the company's objectives of developing teamwork and sharing knowledge.

Comment: Clearly more could be said on all of the above, but this must be balanced against the time constraints placed upon the candidate.

# Specimen answers

## PDS People Resourcing practice examination – Section B

### Question I

> My understanding of how we consider the issue of knowledge management is briefly laid out below. There was an article in *People Management* entitled 'Human Capital: a thorough evaluation' (April 2002) that is worthy of a read.

Definition: Concerned with people and the interchange of knowledge.
*Five ways of supporting knowledge management:*

1 Help to develop an open culture.

2 Promote a climate of commitment and trust.

3 Advise on the design of organisations that support the above.

4 Advise on resourcing policies that attract the people with appropriate skills and attributes.

5 Advise on methods of motivating people to share the knowledge – reward people within the appraisal/reward framework for sharing knowledge.

*[Author's comment:* Added to the above five elements candidates could choose from those below:

• Develop the performance management process, which supports the sharing of knowledge.

• Develop processes for staff development that encourage knowledge transfer.

• With IT (information technology), develop systems for capturing and codifying knowledge.]

## Question 2

How can we improve the position in the NHS with respect to midwives' retention and recruitment? Consider this in two stages, the long-term and the short-term:

- Long-term would involve attraction and retention to the service. Attraction is associated with salary and conditions of work. The government is currently negotiating new salary against modernisation of processes as detailed in the government's paper on the NHS 'Agenda for Change'. Currently salary negotiations are out of the hands of the local NHS Trust. However, the Trust can affect how it recruits within its catchment zone by considering whether it is tapping all available sources, such as targeted campaigns to contact ethnic groups. Internally consideration could be (and is being) given to cross train mature staff. Consideration could also be given to the role of the midwife. Could, for example, parts of the job effectively be devolved into a lesser-qualified role?

- The immediate problems can be addressed by considering what pool of qualified staff are 'potentially available' to the Trust and how it can attract them back to work and hold on to them.

It has been suggested that there has been significant turnover of midwives in recent years. If turnover has been high, then why have people left? Could it be the unsocial hours, non-family policies and practices? There is a requirement to have a system that also finds out why staff are leaving.

The introduction of flexible working practices, coupled with the new salary package and offer of pensionable employment, may encourage staff back into the profession from both agency work and from those parents who have left to bring up children. As a stopgap, recruitment from overseas for such positions is also an option.

Critical to the improvement of morale is a concerted effort to bring the staff shortage under control.

The strategy to improve staff morale should focus on involvement techniques. Techniques that would strengthen the psychological contract between the employer and employee include the management style – move away from the autocratic style of management; consider new styles of working and perhaps move to more involved ways of working; take opportunities to consider methods of working – job enrichment, e.g. flexible teamworking, perhaps self-managed teams. The implication here would be a move from telling, shouldering the burden to facilitating, co-ordinating, sharing responsibility. Clearly, there will be a training and development requirement.

- For staff there will be a need to learn to work in teams and all that this implies. Consideration of leadership techniques, budgeting and managing processes of work. Clearly, there will be a training and development requirement.

Also worth considering are: flexible times of working; developing a new appraisal system focusing on realistic objective-setting; personal development; improving communication – consultative committee, team briefings, etc.

[*Author's comment:* This is a question where it is possible to 'over-egg' the response, as has been done here! It is important to remember that for each Section B question there is only approximately 8 minutes in which to formulate and make a response.]

## Question 3

### *Measuring and attacking turnover*

Activities associated with the above are a cost in themselves. However, knowing how your business 'works' is important when it comes to adding value. Standard ways of indicating turnover are given in Stephen Taylor's book, *People Resourcing*, where he talks about:

- Wastage index
- Stability index

Each is a way at looking at the problem from a slightly different angle. The wastage index is the crudest:

= (Leaver over 12 month period/Total staff) x 100%.

The stability index is a little subtler, seeking to consider only those staff who have remained in post for (usually) 12 months – this

acknowledges the fact that the highest turnover occurs within the
first 12-month period:

> = (Number of staff employed for >12 months)/Original
> number of staff) x 100%.

As Taylor points out, 'a company can have high Wastage and Low
Stability', or as he says, 'worryingly, low wastage and low stability'.
It is important to understand what statistics mean; there are lies,
damned lies and statistics.

### Determining the reasons for leaving

• Exit interviews:

Consideration – Not having the interview conducted by line
management, e.g. 'impartially' by personnel For a number of
reasons this is not the most reliable tool unless, of course, you are
dealing with a very, very honest person. Timing is important –
should be done as soon as the person hands in his/her notice to
leave. Using 'separation questionnaires' – anonymous and may be
done by an impartial contract organisation.

   Useful, in all of the above, is to ask the individual directly how
improvements can be made.

• Attitude surveys:

Rather than closing the door before the horse has bolted it is perhaps
a better idea to survey staff before they take any drastic action – test
the health of the organisation.

*With attitude surveys it is useful to give staff feedback from the results
– and perhaps information as to what the business is going to do about
any areas of concern.*

• Quantitative methods:

Useful for trend analysis, isolating rogue departments sections,
factories. Internal benchmarking. (External benchmarking can be
quite difficult.) It is important to think through the type of statistics,
choosing those that have relevance.

• Surveys of ex-employees:

Currently some large organisations are experimenting with request-
ing ex-employees who have left the organisation to complete questionnaires within a period of months – probably done anonymously
and by a contract agency.

### Reducing staff turnover

The feedback (above) will give clues to a longer-term response to high turnover. The short-term reduction of staff turnover can be achieved in three ways:

- By recruiting people who best fit the company mould and can work alone, and those who are comfortable in their own company and confident about their own abilities.

- By offering greater flexibility of working to existing staff.

- By targeting ethnic groups, or perhaps unusual pools of potential talent (homeless, ex-offenders – see *People Management* article, Nov. 2002, about the Marks and Spencer initiative in working with homeless people to bring them into the world of work).

## Question 4

Treating or perceiving the overall character of an individual in a positive or negative way results in a characteristic specified as positive Halo, negative Horns effect. We are also subject to 'stereotyping' individuals – e.g. all asylum seekers are terrorists.

Managers should be aware of these 'traps' to logical decision-making. The HR professional should properly brief those involved in the interview of the pitfalls of one's perceptions as described above. The interviewer should seek out facts.

The dangers for management are twofold. Firstly, that the wrong people are recruited, or promoted, because decisions were not made objectively, perhaps because there was no challenge process in place. The results of this type of error may not be instantaneous but the outcome of such a poor decision-making process is reduced efficiency and possibly low staff morale. Secondly, there is the issue of discrimination/non-compliance with the relative sex, race or disability Acts – should there be a clear biasing in the selection process, whether this is intentional or unintentional. The latter opens the door to costly litigation and a blemished reputation.

## Question 5

The Data Protection Act has been extended to cover all types of information, whether electronic or hard copy data.

With respect to recruitment and selection:

- Care with the application form – a one-size-fits-all may not be acceptable; the form may have to be designed to fit the recruitment activity. If age is immaterial, then why include this as a request for information?

- Feedback from third parties (references) should only be requested with the full knowledge of the candidate – to ask the general question 'can we approach your previous employer?' may not be good enough.

- References – the DPA covers information sent and received. It is therefore a contravention of the Act to disclose the contents of a reference (usually given in confidence) to a third party. It would also be the breaking of a psychological contract of trust.

- It is good practice to nominate someone as 'responsible' to ensure compliance with the Act and associated company policies.

## Question 6

In respect of good practice when managing our International staff the key considerations should be:

- The reasons why the expatriation is necessary – is the posting simply because of a technical requirement or is it a development posting, etc.? Candidates should be clear why they are being asked to go overseas.

- Cultural acclimatisation – before and on arrival at the overseas location.

- The compatibility of the expatriate's partner to cope with an international assignment. The majority of failures of expatriations are associated with some form of discontent on behalf of an accompanying partner. (Refer to the studies conducted by Sparrow et al. of Sheffield University for the CIPD (*Globalisation and HR*) and also Black et al. (1999), *Globalizing people through international assignments*.)

- Limited-term assignments.

- Financial rewards/compensation.

- Realignment on the expatriate's return to the UK.

• Availability of support from home country while on assignment – mentor, administrative link, etc.

Expatriate compensation should be 'well thought through' and be considered as part of a holistic expatriation package.

*[Author's comment:* Candidates can write much on this subject. The task is to say just sufficient. There are a number of core texts on expatriation issues, which reflect good practice. A good place to start is the CIPD's own study on expatriation practices.]

## Question 7

The following will be significant shaping factors over the next five to 10 years. Refer to Barbara Senior's book, *Organisational change.*

Probably there will be continued impact of globalisation, a general decline in the work ethic and an increased interest from employees and other stakeholders (government, especially a Labour government) in work/life balance. This is already apparent in recent (April 2003) legislation about family-friendly policies. The demographic trends will put pressures on recruitment, causing businesses to look more closely at hitherto overlooked pools of talent (ex-offenders, the unemployed, overseas). Further pressure will be caused by the general decline in population growth (zero), which will cause business to consider the options in engaging further an ageing population. Innovative practices must be employed – extending the retirement age, reducing restrictions on pension law etc. Having and encouraging diversity in the workplace will be key to success – further ethnic, sex or age integration, all coupled with greater flexibility.

## Question 8

Appraisals are about:

• Assessing past performance against previously set targets (linked to the business plan).

• Appraising performance, which can then be turned into reward measures.

• Setting future targets, hard and soft (linked to the balanced score card)

- Associating some hard targets with output appraisal. More difficult to assess are targets associated with the softer, behavioural skills. These may be assessed through critical incident, customer feedback, peer feedback (360-degree feedback in essence).

- Determining learning and development needs: refer to Beardwell and Holden 2001.

Criticisms about my own (imaginary scenario, in this case) organisation:
My biggest concern is that our management does not see/appreciate the importance of the appraisal. Typically, appraisal is conducted in a ritualistic manner: another box to tick against which I, as a manager, am being assessed. There is a lack of ownership by management: the whole process is seen to owned by HR and driven by HR. I would be happier to see that this be turned on its head and the process be clearly owned by management but perhaps administered and facilitated by HR. The current process is not adding to the business performance but, in its present form, adding to the administrative burden and so costing the business.

### Question 9

No selection method is entirely accurate, and some are better than others. The following is a rough guide to the accuracy of prediction:

- Assessment centre (promotion)

- Assessment centre performance coupled with personality tests.

The assessment centre is costly and time-consuming, so is not broadly used. However, the skilled practitioner can embed in the programme psychometric exercises for a number of attributes ranging from personality traits and numerical aptitude to ability. Key, though, is linking the assessment centre to the company's core behavioural skills

- Work sample tests – in terms of the validity, sits between the two types of assessment centre.

Work sample tests, in a similar way, show the way for a candidate to get an understanding of the work process and for him/her also to make a judgement whether the work is appealing. Recruitment and selection is a two-way process.

• Biodata

• Structured interview

Biodata is reliant upon large blocks of data about individuals who have made successes in particular jobs and careers. First used by the American Navy for determining the most suitable persons to become deep-sea divers.

Interviews and application forms are still significantly used by business, although research shows that their reliability is questionable. Stephen Taylor argues that although the classic trio of application form plus interview and references is questionably accurate too radical a change may cause problems for candidates.

Because jobs change, as time goes by, Taylor argues that it is better to screen people out who are lazy, lacklustre and dishonest and to recruit for attitude (difficult to work with – don't fit the culture) and ability (one may say potential).

## Question 10

The government's concern is about the need for local authorities to consider a broader church of attributes when considering people for jobs, including:

• Behavioural questions in the selection process in order to test customer focus and orientation.

• Induction, training and development that concentrate on customer-facing behaviours.

• Reward and recognition systems that reflect achievement and the departmental goals, objectives and strategies.

• Role modelling and leadership from management.

• Involvement techniques to improve employee commitment.

A number of organisations consider the philosophy of 'select for attitude and train for skills'.

## END OF EXAMINATION

# SECTION 4

## CONCLUSION

# 5 CONCLUSION

If you have read this book from cover to cover, you have picked up a raft of invaluable lessons not only about how to prepare for and approach the People Resourcing examination, but also about the principles that should govern your professional priorities as an HR practitioner. Just in case some of the key messages may have been lost in all the 'noise' of the text as a whole, here they are again. Indeed, I find to my pleasure and delight that they all fit neatly into a 'PEOPLE RESOURCING' acronym.

## P

*P is for Purchase.* Buy a copy of Stephen Taylor's CIPD textbook, *People resourcing* (2nd edition, 2002). You will not regret it: the investment will repay itself many times over (but only, of course, if you read the book having purchased it – merely possessing it will not be sufficient). In this revision guide we have consistently emphasised that you cannot pass the People Resourcing examination merely by studying the revision guide on its own: the revision guide is chiefly about methodology, whereas *People resourcing* is about content. As a bonus, Stephen Taylor is a very readable writer.

## E

*E is for Equipment.* Equip yourself with the necessary facilities for systematic study: a quiet place to work, without distractions, a table or a desk positioned so that you cannot look out of the window, a straight-backed chair (soft armchairs are not conducive to disciplined reading), and some earplugs if you need to cut out ambient noise. If you live with others (like flat-sharers or family members), make deals with them to leave you alone when you need to concentrate, at agreed times of the day or week.

## O

*O is for Organisation.* Organise your sequence of one-hour 'active reading' sessions when you sit down (in your straight-backed chair, at your desk or table) and focus on successive key chapters in Stephen Taylor's textbook. Make notes of key points; highlight quotations; underline references; note how Taylor integrates his own thoughts with those of others, because this is exactly the style you must cultivate, partially for the examination, for the assignment, for the major project – and also for your professional duties. You should timetable at least three of these one-hour 'active reading' sessions each week – do not make them longer than 60 minutes, because your concentration will wander.

# P

*P is for Political, Persuasion and Presentation skills*. These are competencies you should develop, again not only for purposes of the examination but also to enable you to advance your career through careful networking and diplomacy. When writing a case study report that is addressed to your (imaginary) chief executive, it is not a good idea to boldly recommend that the chief executive should be dismissed for incompetence: far better to suggest that he/she should move into the newly-created role of company 'president'.

# L

*L is for Looking around*. Whenever you get the chance, deliberately seek out chances to look at how PR is handled in other organisations and, better still, in other business sectors; and see what you can learn from the way they do things. Remember that the CIPD qualification is meant to prepare you for a professional role in any sort of enterprise in any business or economic sector, so it is helpful to learn as much as possible about what goes on elsewhere. Arrange exchange visits with your fellow students; search corporate websites for information (especially those for organisations which operate online recruitment processes, like Asda); investigate the *People Management* archive for articles about world-class organisations like BMW, First Direct, Pret a Manger, and so forth. Download everything that looks interesting and valuable: the broader your knowledge and understanding base, the more impressive your examination answers can be.

# E

*E is for Enthusiasm*. In your examination answers, radiate enthusiasm and a positive mentality. Do not come across to the examiners as cynical, negative and destructive: this is no way for a true professional to behave. This is not to say, however, that you must never be critical: of course you should be critical, because that is the necessary backcloth to continuous improvement. It is being critical without suggesting changes; that is unhelpful – and it is unhelpful for you to act like that at work, too.

## R

*R is for Recommendations*. When asked to produce recommendations (for example, as part of a case study treatment, or as part of a briefly stated scenario in Section B), you must do so – and your recommendations should be clear, precise, unambiguous and businesslike. Vague exhortations to introduce a performance management scheme will not be welcomed, nor will any proposals that are advanced uncertainly or diffidently, using words like 'hopefully' or formulations like 'management should consider the introduction of performance-related incentive schemes'. The examiners may not like some of your recommendations, but you will always receive credit if they are articulated vigorously and defended strongly.

## E

*E is for the Examination*. There is no need for panic as you approach the examination. The only people who panic are those who (a) have not prepared themselves adequately, and (b) have no practised adequately. If you prepare yourself conscientiously, and submit yourself to some practice sessions in order to acquire examination skills and techniques, then you will feel an enormous surge of self-confidence that in turn will stimulate your performance in the examination itself. Examinations are like interviews: the more you do, the better you get at them.

## S

*S is for Strategic orientation*. In your approach to your role, and to the examination, you should consciously adopt a 'big picture' mentality in which you seek to understand why the organisation acts as it does, why its priorities are what they are, against the structure of its strategic goals, its vision, mission and values. If your responses to PR questions are entirely focused on operational, process and procedural issues (for example, the design of an appraisal form, rather than the objectives for the appraisal process), then almost certainly you will fail.

# O

*O is for Opportunity.* The examination is an opportunity, not a problem. It is an opportunity for you to sell yourself (metaphorically speaking) to the examiners and through them to the CIPD. Seize every opportunity in the examination to demonstrate what you know, what you can do with what you know, and what you think about what you know. If your answers do not contain any references to third-party authors, researchers or literature sources, the examiners may legitimately conclude that you have not read anything – and will mark your answers accordingly.

# U

*U is for Understanding.* One of the key criteria in the BACKUP formula is the necessity for you to show that you are capable of critical understanding within each of the major themes in the learning objectives and indicative content. This means that your answer material must go beyond the mere reproduction of 'facts', but must incorporate a critical assessment of the facts and even the capacity to challenge 'facts' that appear to have little or new empirical support. For example, it is commonly argued that one-to-one selection interviews are 'subjective', whereas panel interviews are 'objective'. There is no evidence to support this claim: it rests entirely on conventional wisdom. Indeed, the world of PR is replete with similar instances that deserve to be, at the very least, reviewed.

# R

*R is for Reflection.* When you are at work, or when you are reading Stephen Taylor's book, or when you are attending a PR class, reflect on your experiences: think about them, assess their significance for you, and store them away in your memory box of learning. Where you can, consider the wider implications of what is happening or what you observe taking place around you, so that, for example, the treatment of a job applicant is interpreted against the background of emotional intelligence (either the display of EQ or its lack).

# C

*C is for CPD (Continuing Professional Development) and also for Competencies.* CPD is vital to your progress and development, as it is for the examiners themselves. You should keep a learning log and regularly (at least once a month) transfer information into your CPD file. Also, you should assess yourself against each of the 10 competencies linked to the CIPD's Professional Development Scheme, and establish personal development plans to address any perceived deficiencies. (If you are not sure whether your performance is deficient against any of the 10 competencies, ask some of your colleagues, your boss, and if you have some, your staff: they will soon tell you what your strengths and weaknesses are.)

# I

*I is for Irritant.* In your own organisation, and in class sessions, keep asking questions – do not just sit there and accept what you're told. At work, if anything you are asked to do seems senseless, or you want a justification for it, then ask; ask 'Why do we ...?' and 'Why don't we ...?' about procedures, processes and systems that at first might appear not to add value. Asking questions is a symptom of the positive learner – although it will make you unwelcome in some quarters. Never mind: keep at it, always remembering to ask your questions politely and courteously.

# N

*N is for New.* You must keep up to date, and switched on to any significant emergent topics within the PR arena, like employer branding, online recruitment and outsourcing. This means you should study every issue of *People Management* from cover to cover, and retain any articles, features or news items that are relevant to your interests. File these pieces of information away in your personal concertina file, with compartments labelled in accordance with the major sections of the indicative content. Go through the file as a central part of your pre-examination revision.

# G

*G is for Goals.* It is always a mistake to satisfice when preparing for this or any other examination, that is, to do what you judge to be just enough work to enable you to get by with a mark of 50 per cent. Although the examination is a comprehensive test of your capabilities, you may find on the day that one or two of the questions will concern topics of which you know little, and so you will fail. Whereas, aiming for a mark of 60 per cent will give you a safety margin – and will, like practice with examinations (see above), give you the additional strength of self-confidence that is so valuable during the examination itself.

Thank you for reading the *People resourcing* revision guide. All that remains is for you to turn intention into reality. Please do so.

# APPENDIX

## Performance Standards

### Purpose

The pace of change affecting organisations shows no sign of slowing down, and has strong impact on managerial expectations about:

- employee behaviour and attitudes

- corporate pressures on managerial performance

- the employability potential and aspirations of labour market entrants

- the criteria for success applied to those engaged in employee resourcing activities.

Therefore, this module is designed to recognise the following key points:

- For any organisation to achieve its People Resourcing (PR) outcomes the PR professional must be aware of the organisation's strategic direction and be able to demonstrate that the resourcing policies, systems and procedures contribute to achieving the corporate strategic goals.

- There is no guarantee that today's organisations will exist in the indefinite future, either at all or in their present form. So this module seeks to address the competencies resourcing professionals are likely to need 'everywhere and tomorrow', rather than just the 'here and now'.

- Administering employment systems in line with the law and recognised standards of fairness and good practice is important, but it does not make the difference between success and failure in the marketplace. PR professionals add real value through their contribution to the recruitment, selection, deployment, development and retention of people who themselves add value to the organisation, individually and collectively.

Many employers still use recruitment and selection processes for which there is little or no supporting evidence. The talents and potential of people are often dissipated or neglected, poor performers are still ignored, sidelined, promoted or dismissed without any serious attempt to resolve the problem, and performance review systems generate passionate debate because they appear unable to generate significant benefits for the organisation or the employee. Many of those engaged in employee resourcing concentrate on minor incremental efficiency or system changes and on the legalistic, ethical and procedural dimensions of resourcing – instead of on the added-value dimension, where there is considerable scope for further improvement.

• The competent practitioner has to be familiar with the major tools and techniques related to PR, and also be able to assess the potential for using them, determine their suitability for specific organisational scenarios, implement them with and through the co-operation of other stakeholders, evaluate their effectiveness and carry out any necessary modifications.

This module crucially sets out to develop, demonstrate and assess these capabilities.

## Performance indicators

### Operational indicators

Practitioners must be able to:

1. Make constructive contributions to the development or enhancement of People Resourcing (PR) policies.

2. Evaluate existing PR processes, systems and procedures, and propose cost-effective improvements.

3. Optimise the use of available tools and techniques in the field of IT (including the Internet) for all aspects of PR.

4. Assist with the design, development, implementation and review of PR methods to resolve specific corporate scenarios (representative examples are: geographical relocation, new

business development, management of an acquisition, corporate restructuring, graduate expatriate appointments, delayering, devolution, decentralisation, retrenchment, and using an outsourcing partner such as a recruitment agency).

5.  Undertake the full range of day-to-day functions for which a PR professional generally is accountable (for example, recruitment, performance, reward, retention, release).

6.  Contribute to the development of human resource plans that relate to and help achieve business/corporate goals.

7.  Critically evaluate existing PR systems and new approaches or methodologies.

8.  Co-operate positively with executive managerial stakeholders – 'customers' – in the design and implementation of resourcing processes.

9.  Advocate and secure compliance with all appropriate ethical and legal obligations associated with PR.

10. Apply the principles and practice of Continuing Professional Development for their own personal development.

## Knowledge indicators

Practitioners must understand and be able to explain:

1.  The underpinning rationale for PR as a means for accomplishing corporate purposes, strategies and goals through people.

2.  The environmental context in which PR is designed, operated, reviewed and improved.

3.  The benefits, limitations and potential of existing and emerging methodologies in the generic field of PR.

4.  The legal obligations governing the creation and use of all PR strategies, policies, procedures and systems.

5.  Ethicality criteria for all key aspects of PR, including the benefits of compliance and the risks associated with its neglect.

6.  The systematic approach to PR, from the creation of a cost-effective

human resource plan, through recruitment, selection, socialisation, training/development, performance management, retention and review, to eventual employee release.

7.  The nature, purposes, features, applications, benefits and disadvantages of the principal techniques for human resource planning, recruitment, selection, corporate socialisation and people performance.

8.  The operational need for pragmatic PR programmes, in circumstances of organisational turbulence, crisis, closure or apocalyptic change.

9.  New developments in PR and their application potential.

10. Contingency factors that influence the principles and practice of PR across and within various employment sectors.

## Indicative content

### 1. PR in context

The changing world of work and organisations:

1.  The big picture: contextual themes relevant to PR (such as globalisation, privatisation, ecological/environmental concerns, technological innovation, accelerating 'customer' expectations, competitive intensity and demographic change).

2.  The corporate picture: evolving employer expectations about employee behaviour and attitudes, with special reference to 'adding value' obligations; new forms of work contract; the PR significance of organisational transience.

3.  The people picture: the future for the work ethic; processes of vocational choice; the job/career dichotomy; the concept of 'employability' and its implications.

### 2. The strategic significance of PR

1.  The PR function: the key role of people as contributors to the realisation of corporate purposes, strategies and goals.

2.  The 'customers' for PR: establishing priorities between various

stakeholders and 'customers; creating, sustaining and developing partnerships with internal and external stakeholders such as:

- managers with devolved accountabilities for PR
- outsourced contractors
- recruitment agencies and executive search consultants.

3. Managing their possibly conflicting competing concerns, values and expectations.

### 3. Approaches to PR

1. The traditional paradigm: a coherent corporate strategy leading to effective human resource planning, recruitment and selection, induction, training and development, performance review management, employee retention, recognition and reward and release (voluntary or not).

2. New paradigms: the development of aspirational visions for people performance, contribution and commitment; systems that convert these visions into reality; PR practices in the organic enterprise.

3. Contingency-based PR: the specific features of PR processes that typically exist in each principal occupational sector (private/public/not-for-profit); variations from the traditional paradigm (for example, for deliberately transient structures, in environments of extreme turbulence, or circumstances of organisational crisis).

### 4. Human resource planning

1. The rationale for human resource planning: its potential benefits, disadvantages and dangers.

2. Designing, implementing and reviewing the effectiveness of a human resource plan: the use of appropriate measures, for example, employee retention, turnover, productivity, and profitability-per-employee.

3. Internal and external factors affecting human resource planning and implementation including:

- trends in the labour market (both supply and demand)
- competitor practices
- technological change
- political initiatives
- the social background
- enhanced customer expectations
- strategic clarity and consistency within the organisation
- corporate politics and the distribution of power.

### 5. Recruitment and selection

1.  The background to recruitment and selection: criteria for administering the process efficiently and effectively; alternative approaches to managing vacancies; job analysis; job descriptions versus accountability profiles; person specifications versus competency frameworks.

2.  The recruitment process: the principal methods available – their features, benefits and disadvantages (for example, media advertising, the Internet, employment agencies, executive search consultancies).

3   The selection process: the principal techniques available – their features, benefits and disadvantages (for example, interviewing, individual group simulation exercises, and psychometrics).

4.  Measuring the effectiveness of recruitment and selection: techniques for monitoring outcomes to ensure continued business relevance, validity, reliability, and compliance: continuous improvement processes in recruitment and selection.

### 6. People management

Optimising commitment and performance:

1.  Assimilating people into the organisation: the socialisation/induction process, transmitting corporate values and behavioural parameters.

2.  Developing and improving performance: the benefits and limitations of appraisal; criteria for effective performance feedback; coaching, mentoring and other systems for achieving a productive balance between the employee's needs and the employer's requirements.

3.  Dealing with performance issues: assessing the nature and causes of performance problems (for example, absence, attitude, capability or output); the range of remedies/solutions available; techniques for implementing action and monitoring consequences.

4.  Motivating people: the elements of job design; the principles underpinning cost-effective reward and recognition strategies.

5   Keeping people: practical policies for employee retention and commitment, especially where long-term employment is not guaranteed.

6.  Releasing people: the effective management of strategies, policies, systems and processes for retirement, redundancy, dismissal, and voluntary turnover; mechanisms for preventing or alleviating problems where appropriate.

### 7. Special-case scenarios

PR policies, plans, processes and systems for particular (possibly short-term) corporate exigencies. Representative examples are:

*   recruiting expatriates (temporary or permanent) or graduates

*   choosing outsourcing agencies or recruitment consultants

*   creating (new) shift-work teams and patterns

*   resolving resource problems in times of acute labour scarcity

*   establishing new corporate entities arising from mergers or acquisitions.

### 8. Support tools for effective PR

1.  The nature, scope, costs, benefits and applications of information technology (including the Internet) for recruitment, selection and the retention/retrieval of employee data.

2.  External sources of information, advice and assistance, including the CIPD, published research and benchmarking indices.

### 9. Compliance and ethicality obligations in PR

1.  The place of legal, ethical and professional compliance as a 'critical failure factor' for PR practitioners and their employers.

2.  The legal constraints and frameworks relevant to PR.

3.  The influence of legal and quasi-legal directives originating through the European Union and elsewhere.

4.  Ethicality expectations within each major dimension of PR, including diversity management, equal opportunities and discrimination.

5.  Professionalism criteria: CIPD Codes of Conduct and publications from other sources.

### 10. PR: the future

[*Note*: Practitioners – like practitioners in any discipline who are actively engaged in Continuing Professional Development – are expected to be up to date with emerging PR issues. The four here are representative examples only.]

1.  Debates over the future of work and employment, especially in view of continuing technological change, globalisation and the growth of e-commerce.

2.  The dilemma of seeking to reconcile the interests and preferences of individual employees with the requirements and expectations of organisations.

3.  New thinking and research on topics relevant to PR, such as:

    •   matching personality types or learning styles with specific occupational roles

    •   the effectiveness of psychometric tests

    •   emotional intelligence

    •   knowledge management.

4.  Actual and potential developments in employment legislation and other compliance arenas.

# REFERENCES, FURTHER READING AND WEBSITES

## References

BEARDWELL, I. and HOLDEN, L. (2001) *Human resource management: a contemporary approach.* Harlow: FT Prentice Hall.

BUCKINGHAM, M. (2001) What a waste. *People Management,* 11 October.

BURNES, B. *Change management.* Harlow: FT Prentice Hall.

CORBRIDGE, M. and PILBEAM, S. (1998) *Employment resourcing.* London: FT Publishing.

CULLY, M., WOODLAND, S., O'REILLY, A. and DIX, G. (2002) *Britain at work, as depicted by the 1998 workplace employee relations survey.* London: Routledge.

*ECONOMIST.* (2003) Business in bad times, 5 April.

FRIEDMAN, M. (1963) *Capitalism and freedom.* Chicago: University of Chicago Press.

HUCZYNSKI, A. and BUCHANAN, D. (2001) *Organizational behaviour: an introductory text.* Harlow: FT Prentice Hall.

JOYNT, P. and MORTON, B. (2000) *The global HR manager.* London: CIPD.

MINTZBERG, H. (1994) *The rise and fall of strategic planning.* New York: Prentice Hall.

PFEFFER, J. and SUTTON, R. (1999) *The knowing-doing gap: how smart companies turn knowledge into action.* Boston: Harvard Business School Press.

PORTER, M. and KETELS, J. (2003) *UK competitiveness: moving to the next stage.* London: Department of Trade and Industry Economic Paper No. 3.

SENIOR, B. (2002) *Organisational change.* Harlow: FT Prentice Hall.

STOREY, J. (2001) *Human resource management: a critical text.* London: Thomson Learning.

*SUNDAY TIMES* (2004) Grey power plugs jobs market by D. Smith, 18 January.

TAYLOR, S. (2002) *People resourcing.* 2nd edn. London: CIPD.

*THE TIMES* (2004) Pipe and slippers? Not just yet by R. Miles, 22 March.

TORRINGTON, D., HALL, L. and TAYLOR, S. (2002) *Human resource management*. Harlow: FT Prentice Hall.

## Further reading

ARMSTRONG, M. (2002) *A handbook of human resources management practice*. London: Kogan Page.

BACH, S. and SISSONS, K. (2002) *Personnel management: a comprehensive guide to theory and practice*. Oxford: Blackwell.

BLACK, J.S., GREGERSEN, H.B., MENDENHALL, M.E. and STROH, L.K. (1999) *Globalizing people through international assignments*. Addison Wesley Longman.

BRATTON, J. and GOLD, J. (2003) *Human resources management theory and practice*. 3rd edn. Basingstoke: Palgrave.

GRANT, B. (2002) *Employment law*. London: Thomson Learning.

HERZBERG, F. (1968) One more time: how do you motivate employees? *Harvard Business Review* (reprinted December 2003).

PILBEAM, S. and CORBRIDGE, M. (2002) *People resourcing: HRM in practice*. Harlow: FT Prentice Hall.

WALTON, J. (1999) *Strategic human resources development*. Harlow: FT Prentice Hall.

### CIPD research papers

BEAUMONT, P.B. and HUNTER, L.C. (2002) *Managing knowledge workers*. London: CIPD.

BREWSTER, C. SPARROW, P. and HARRIS, H. (2002) *Globalisation and HR*. London: CIPD.

COUSEY, M. (2000) *Getting the right work–life balance*. London: CIPD.

HARRIS, H., BREWSTER, C. and SPARROW, P. (2001) *HR and globalisation*. London: CIPD.

PURCELL J., KINNIE N., HUTCHINSON S., RAYTON B. and SWART J. (2003). *Understanding the people performance link: unlocking the black box.* London: CIPD.

SCARBROUGH, H. and ELIAS, J. (2002) *Evaluating human capital*. London: CIPD.

SCARBROUGH, H. (2002) *Investigating knowledge management.* London: CIPD.

SWART, J., KINNIE, N. AND PURCELL, J. (2003) *People and performance in knowledge-intensive firms.* London: CIPD.

Managing employee careers: issues, trends and prospects. *Survey Report.* June 2003. London: CIPD.

**CIPD Change Agendas**

DONKIN, R. (2004) *HR and reorganization: managing the challenge of change.* London: CIPD.

RUTHERFORD, A. and PULLEN, R. (2003) *Religious discrimination and introduction to the law.* London: CIPD.

SCARBROUGH, H. (2003) *Human capital: external reporting framework.* London: CIPD.

CIPD (2003) *The challenge of the age.* London: CIPD.

SKAPINKER, M. (2002) *Knowledge management.* London: CIPD.

**CIPD Guides**

*International mergers and acquisitions* (2003) London: CIPD.

**CIPD Survey Reports**

*HR and expatriation trends* (2002) London: CIPD.

*Managing employee careers: issues, trends and prospects* (2003) London: CIPD.

*Recruitment, retention and turnover* (2004) London: CIPD.

# Useful websites

**ACAS:** www.acas.org.uk/

### Age discrimination

'**Age Positive**': www.agepositive.gov.uk
A team working in the Department for Work and Pensions in Sheffield and London, responsible for strategy and policies to support people making decisions about working and retirement. The Age Positive campaign promotes the benefits of employing a

mixed-age workforce that includes older and younger people. The objective is to encourage employers to make decisions about recruitment, training and retention that do not discriminate against someone because of their age. They use publications, research, press, events and awards initiatives to get the message across – and to help employers prepare for legislation in 2006 to outlaw age discrimination in employment.

**CIPD:** www.cipd.co.uk/
  www.peoplemanagement.co.uk/

**Employment law:** www.emplaw.co.uk/
**Institute of Employment Studies:** www.employment-studies.co.uk
**Confederation of British Industry (CBI)**: www.cbi.org.uk
  'The online voice of British Industry'

### Drugs and alcohol

**Alcoholics Anonymous**: www.alcoholics-anonymous.org.uk
**Alcohol Concern**: www.alcoholconcern.org.uk
**Narcotics Anonymous**: www.ukna.org

**Engineering Employers Federation (EEF)**: www.eef.org.uk & www.eef.co.uk
The EEF is the largest employers' association covering engineering, manufacturing and technology-based industries. It gives a wide range of professional advice on HR, legal, education, health and safety, training and skills.

**Equal Opportunities Commission**: www.eoc.org.uk/
**European Union:** www.europa.eu.int/

### Government and industry

**Acts of Parliament, UK general**: www.hmso.gov.uk/acts.htm
**Criminal Records Bureau (CRB)**: www.crb.gov.uk
The role of the CRB, as defined by the Home Office Minister: 'The role of the Criminal Records Bureau is to reduce the risk of abuse by ensuring that those who are unsuitable are not able to work with children and vulnerable adults.'

**Data Protection Act**: www.dataprotection.gov.uk
**Government Direct**: www.direct.gov.uk
Provides gateway access to most government and other reputable websites.
**Health and Safety Executive:** www.hse.gov.uk
**Learning and Skills Council:** www.lsc.gov.uk/
**Thinking, initiatives and support:** www.dti.gov.uk
**UK Government Statistics:** www.statistics.gov.uk/

**Investors in People:** www.iipuk.co.uk/
**International Labour Organisation:** www.ilo.org/
Useful website from drugs to statistics.

### Recruitment

**Association of Online Recruiters:** www.aolr.org/

*Graduate careers and job opportunities*

**Association of Graduate Recruiters:** www.agr.org.uk and www.prospects.ac.uk
This is the website for the Higher Education Careers Service Unit. It describes itself as Britain's 'official graduate website' and offers a search facility for 'hundreds of graduate job vacancies'.

*Specialist graduate recruitment websites*

**Getalife:** www.getalife.org.uk
A specialist site that gives access to graduate job opportunities and careers guidance information. It is backed by Graduate Prospects, promoting graduate opportunities in the public sector.
**Doctorjob**: www.doctorjob.com
A commercial website focusing on graduate recruitment activities. It claims to be the number one graduate recruiting website.

**MaturityWorks**: www.maturityworks.co.uk
A recently launched commercial web recruitment initiative that focuses exclusively on the needs and interests of older workers – and the organisations who increasingly need to recruit them.

**Trades Union Congress**: www.tuc.org.uk

**Working Families (formally Parents at Work)**: www.working families.org.uk
A charity dealing with advice for families and employers about work–life balance and related issues.

### Statistics, trends

**International Labour Statistics, International Labour Office**: http://laborsta.ilo.org
**Workplace Employment Relations Survey (WERS 2004)**: access from the DTI website: www.dti.gov.uk/er
A national survey of people at work. The survey is jointly sponsored by the Department of Trade and Industry, the Advisory, Conciliation and Arbitration Service, the Economic and Social Research Council, and the Policy Studies Institute. Earlier surveys were conducted in 1980, 1984, 1990 and 1998.

The purpose of each survey in the series has been to provide large-scale, statistically reliable evidence about a broad range of industrial relations and employment practices across almost every sector of the economy in Great Britain. This evidence is collected with the following objectives in mind:

- to provide a mapping of employment relations practices in workplaces across Great Britain

- to monitor changes in those practices over time

- to both inform policy development and permit an informed assessment of the effects of public policy

- to bring about a greater understanding of employment relations as well as the labour market.

To that end, the survey collects information from: managers with responsibility for employment relations or personnel matters; trade union or employee representatives; and employees themselves.

# INDEX